195

W9-AHF-911

DOGS
and
KIDS

DOGS
and
KIDS

Parenting Tips

Bardi McLennan

With photographs by
Shon Cox Doucette

New York

Maxwell Macmillan Canada
Toronto

Maxwell Macmillan International
New York   Oxford   Singapore   Sydney

Copyright © 1993 by Bardi McLennan

All rights reserved. No part of this book may be reproduced or transmitted in any form or by any means, electronic or mechanical, including photocopying, recording, or by any information storage and retrieval system, without permission in writing from the Publisher.

Howell Book House
Macmillan Publishing Company
866 Third Avenue
New York, NY 10022

Maxwell Macmillan Canada, Inc.
1200 Eglinton Avenue East
Suite 200
Don Mills, Ontario M3C 3N1

Macmillan Publishing Company is part of the Maxwell Communication Group of Companies.

Library of Congress Cataloging-in-Publication Data

McLennan, Bardi.
    Dogs and kids / Bardi McLennan;with photographs by Shon Cox Doucette.
        p.   cm.
    ISBN 0-87605-535-8
    1. Dogs—Training. 2. Dogs—Social aspects. 3. Children and animals. 4. Parenting. I. Title.
    SF431.M466   1993   93-16468   CIP
    636.7′0887—dc20

Macmillan books are available at special discounts for bulk purchases for sales promotions, premiums, fund-raising, or educational use. For details, contact:

Special Sales Director
Macmillan Publishing Company
866 Third Avenue
New York, NY 10022

10 9 8 7 6 5 4 3 2 1

Printed in the United States of America

To Wendy, Gordon and Douglas,
without whom I could never have raised dogs,
and to the likes of Bruce, Cobber, D-B, Bertie,
Badger and Bittersweet, without whom I could never
have raised the kids.

Contents

About the Author

BARDI McLENNAN has owned, bred, rescued, trained, groomed, shown, studied and written about dogs most of her life. Her dog writing career may have begun at age seven with a plea to her sister in England to bring back a ''Cocker Spaneliel.''

For eighteen years she was also editorial assistant to Amy Vanderbilt, whose daily etiquette columns were syndicated in over 200 leading newspapers. She also wrote a series of illustrated etiquette booklets, including one for teenagers, while her children were growing up. After Miss Vanderbilt's sudden death, Bardi continued to write the daily columns and a monthly page in *Ladies' Home Journal* for four years, at which point etiquette was put to bed and all her attention turned entirely to the dogs.

Two years with a call-in radio show answering pet behavioral questions, were followed by The Canine Consultant, a series of six one-hour audio-tapes to guide the pet owner in everything from selecting the right dog to caring (and then grieving) for the aging dog. Everyone, including little children, find the tapes friendly, non-parental and un-complicated.

Bardwyn Kennels, which began in 1966, turned out three of the top-producing Welsh Terrier dogs of their day. Now there was time, too, for writing the script for the AKC video tape on the Welsh Terrier breed, writing a booklet "What Is a Welsh Terrier?" (a guide for would-be owners), judging scores of matches, Specialty Sweepstakes for various breeds coast to coast, speaking to groups ranging from school children to breeders to pet owners to the pet industry, television appearances, solving individual behavioral problems for a multitude of dog owners (for which she has but one rule: never to accept payment) . . . and *always*, writing.

Bardi is immersed in teaching responsible dog ownership, with prevention as the easiest means of combating common behavioral problems in dogs. Her column, "On Good Behavior," appears monthly in *Dog Fancy* magazine. In 1991 her efforts were acknowledged by the Pedigree award for Outstanding Pet Journalist.

Introduction

MUCH OF OUR ENJOYMENT and admiration of animals stems from their childlike characteristics. Excellent wildlife photography lets us enjoy video close-ups of young animals. The playful babylike, round-headed panda, the polar bear cubs sliding down a snowbank, the fox kits playing games now that will mean self-preservation in a year's time, all these babies strike a nurturing note in us. Perhaps because our pet dogs remain in a period of pre-adolescence, it is easier for us to forgive their misbehaviors and justify their presence in our homes. They amuse, beguile and crave our attention in all the ways of a small child.

But, as Stephen Budiansky points out again and again in his book, *The Covenant of the Wild—Why Animals Chose Domestication*, we cannot content ourselves with the charms of animals without accepting them for what they are, or without accepting their complete lives (and therefore our own), which include the entire, not-always-so-charming cycle of birth, life and death.

Dogs were domesticated roughly twelve thousand years ago when they chose to throw in their lot with humans. Dogs became *pets*, or sort of humanized animals, when they were allowed to live in the house, given individual names and never eaten. This change in attitude is credited with being the foundation of both the perception of and our concern with cruelty to all animals, which flowered in the late nineteenth century.

There is a surprising lack of information to be found on the subject of dogs (or any pets, for that matter) in the current crop of books on raising kids. It's as though the world of youngsters extends only as far as the local nursery or day-care center. On the other side of the aisle, there is a similar dearth of information regarding young children in books on dog care; other than a possible reference to bite avoidance. All this despite the statistics which indicate that there are over 54 million dogs in American homes!

I hear from the children in those homes. Sadly, their questions reflect the fact that parents often fail to realize how deep the child's desire is to own a dog, nor do they adequately acknowledge the closeness of the bonds that exist between the kids and their dogs.

A national survey of pet owners showed 32 percent valued their relationships with their dogs as much as those with their best friends. And, shamefully perhaps, 15 percent rated their dogs over their own kids. It would seem that no matter what job we assign to our dogs—hunter, herder, puller of sleds, guardian of property, aid to the less able, best friend, child companion or child substitute—the dogs perform superbly.

Adults are more familiar with the language of parenting kids than they are with the lingo used in discussing how to raise a dog, so *Dogs and Kids* is written in the language of and based on the principles of child parenting.

In the following chapters you'll discover how these parenting principles can be successfully adapted, or sometimes used as is, in raising puppies or in coping with behavior problems in mature dogs, while still allowing them to remain dogs. Parenting works because our dogs—wonderful as they are—are stalled for all their eight to fifteen years in many ways that are roughly equivalent to the needs and behaviors of our pre-school children. The concept works, too, because so many dog owners are parents, or if not, may think of themselves as ''parents'' of a dog. (Take heart! Those special problems that occur in the child-substitute dog relationship are covered, too!)

The dog that becomes the owner's favorite, regardless of the breed, size or potential, is considered by that owner to be smarter and able to communicate better than most other dogs, especially those belonging to friends and neighbors! In 1857, Francis Butler wrote* "To hear some people speak of their pets, one might be led to believe their dogs learned enough to instruct the whole family." He goes on to make another valid and timely point: "The dog in the house knows the varied habits and movements of the inmates, the hour to rise and the hour of retirement, breakfast, dinner and tea; in fact he appears to understand a hundred things he never was taught; whilst the poor beast of a watchdog at the end of his four-foot chain is justly accused of being one of the most untractable, illiterate brutes in creation. Society, habit and example are the sole causes of the difference. Had the pet been on the chain, and the forlorn watchdog inside, the reverse would have been the case."

The life of the dog has not changed at all in this respect. The chained dog remains forlorn and illiterate to this day.

RESPONSIBLE DOG OWNERSHIP

In looking at parenting as an active form of responsible dog ownership, we must never forget that the object of the exercise is a *dog*. To do otherwise is a disservice to the dog. We can utilize our human techniques because that's where *we're* coming from, but to treat the dog, especially the beguiling puppy, as anything more or less than a companion animal, a dog, will bring only disappointment.

Then there are the kids themselves, most of whom either come into this world with a dog in-house or will acquire one later, but all of whom will reap the pleasures, learning experiences and childhood memories of growing up with dogs. Without some guidelines for achieving this idyllic camaraderie, together with warnings as to what can go wrong between dogs and kids, some experiences could be less than wonderful. So we'll discuss ways to prevent a catastrophe even

*Breeding, Training, Management, Diseases, Etc., of Dogs, by Francis Butler (New York: Eckler Printer, 1857).

when the child and dog appear to be geared up for a head-on collision, as well as solutions to numerous other pet/family situations.

Life is neither static nor idyllic, so the topics of separation, divorce, new partners, child custody and death of a pet are discussed realistically, with a modern outlook.

DISCIPLINE

It would be farfetched to say that all forms of child discipline can be applied to dog behaviors. However, there are numerous disciplines that do work precisely because we *want* our pet dogs to behave like "good little children" and to fit into our homes and lives in ways that are socially acceptable to humans.

"Discipline" is the key word because it's currently a high-priority topic with everyone—parents, grandparents, day-care personnel, doctors, teachers—*everyone* involved in the raising of a child from the day it is born. Don't get me wrong, however. I do not, by any stretch of the imagination, propose anthropomorphizing or suggesting that every puppy be raised as a *baby*.

However, the more I studied the new approach to solving (or preventing) behavioral problems in toddlers put forth by a wide range of child psychologists, psychiatrists, pediatricians, parenting counselors and parents themselves, the more it became clear that the behavior perceived as a problem was often the same for both dogs and children (with the same or similar cause and effect) and that the disciplinary procedures for solving them did indeed work as well with dogs as with the young child.

Discipline is guidance, not punishment. It is a method by which we *teach*, and our students (dogs or kids) *learn*. Discipline is what forms the perimeter of acceptable behavior, becoming the security fence to maintain harmony within the family, or in the case of dogs, within the pack.

Discipline is the teaching process. It is the owner's application of disciplining the puppy that harbors the variables. That is why there can be NO ONE RIGHT way or solution that will always work for every person, for every dog. Those variables are numerous, but include:

- Your own personality
- Your lifestyle and that of others in the household
- The dog's age, breed and individual temperament and personality
- How you react to "normal" catastrophes as well as to those generated by the canine persuasion
- Whether or not you ever owned a dog before this, and when, and what kind

Just please don't use any of these things as excuses for unacceptable behavior in your dog. These are only reasons to try another possible course of action when, after a fair trial, the first one proves unsuccessful. Simply because several possible solutions may be offered, this does not mean you should "try everything" in such rapid succession that you give up on one method before the dog has had a chance to learn what you are trying to teach. Follow the tortoise (slow and steady), not the hare!

THE TODDLER AND THE PUPPY, ALIKE IN MANY WAYS

On the street you hold the toddler by the hand, and the puppy on a leash. At home, kitchen cabinets are kept closed because they normally contain things that are dangerous to young kids and young dogs. Also dangerous to both are trash and garbage and any toy or object small enough to fit in the mouth (especially if found on the floor).

Many toddler and puppy behaviors are alike! They share an intense curiosity, the "nine-tenths" law of possession (everything is me! mine!), and on the good side, an insatiable appetite and capacity for learning.

A disciplinary measure that works equally well on child or dog is the Time-Out, which gives the youngster minutes in solitude to contemplate the error of his or her ways. While I won't pretend any dog is going to sit there and try to figure out what's wrong with barking at the mailman, dogs do understand your approval (which they want) and disapproval (which they do not). The Time-Out tells the pup you definitely disapprove of whatever behavior preceded it, and the method has additional preventive advantages that are fully explained. Sometimes we look so hard at the problem, we fail to see the right solution, and sometimes we look for a fancy cure when the best solution is just old-fashioned common sense.

OBEDIENCE, A LEARNING EXPERIENCE

There are references to Obedience class because the classroom (even if in fact it's an open field) is a microcosm of the society in which the dog lives. If the dog's family consists of a single person, then the class provides an extended family of other people, other dogs, other authority. All meet on neutral turf, not the guarded territory of one dog. All are on one end of a leash or the other. All listen. All watch. All learn.

There are good classes and bad ones. The best are interesting (you are told why, not just how), active, fun for you and the dog and use positive training methods, teach things you can use every day. Bad ones are none of the above. Attend as a spectator (without your dog) to form an opinion.

This is a book about life, from introducing the resident dog to a newborn baby, to how to explain to a heartbroken child about the inevitable death of a much-loved pet, to what the future can offer a dog-smitten teenager. It's about everything in between. It's about coping and caring, and teaching and learning, and sharing. It's about our dogs and our kids, and about those dogs we prefer to think of as our kids.

PART ONE

Dogs *as* Kids
Using "Parenting" Techniques

1

The Parenting Principle

DISCIPLINING A CHILD or a dog is not a "one size fits all" solution for behavior, but it *is* the most important aspect of parenting. Good discipline is consistent, it is firm and it is fair.

The basic premise of this book is to tie responsible dog ownership to the principles of "parenting," which has become a crucial course of study not only for 1990s working parents, but for those approaching first-time parenthood in their thirties and forties, and for those without close family role models.

PARENTING A TODDLER AND OWNING A DOG

The parallels between parenting a toddler and the responsibilities of owning a dog are numerous. There's the toddler's basic needs— feeding, grooming, safekeeping, simple teaching and love. The dog's needs are the same. The toddler grows to assume responsibility for many of the basics, but the dog remains trapped for life in a time warp of the young child. Trust and understanding develop between dog and owner, but the principles of parenting stay in effect because the dog's fundamental needs are ongoing.

The currently popular theory that the parents must be trained before successfully training the child is another aspect of parenting that applies to dogs and their owners. Parenting a dog is a lot more involved than teaching the commands *Heel*, *Sit*, *Stand*, *Stay*, *Come* and *Down*, just as parenting a child is infinitely more than teaching the ABCs or how to use a knife and fork.

Discipline

Six weeks in an Obedience class will, at best, teach the owner one way to make the dog respond to basic verbal commands. It's a start, and a necessary one, but the dog may have already learned a few other things, too. For example, the pup will have a very good idea of what it can get away with, how soft you are, what buttons to push to make *you* jump. Such classes cannot adequately instruct the owner in how to cope with all the individual behavioral problems that arise at home. And, as you'll see, behavioral problems are more likely to occur at home than away, because that's where your rules are relaxed. Nor can classes prepare the owner for the numerous variations on Obedience routines that puppies can dream up. You think they're doing it to be cute, but that's the puppy's version of "Gotcha!" (The solution? Enjoy a good laugh at the pup's idea of a joke when you retell the story, but by friendly persuasion show the pup how to do it *your* way.)

This brings us to another point. There is NOT ONE RIGHT WAY to discipline or to handle the problems you and your dog will encounter, so you will find in these pages suggestions for alternative solutions that will allow for breed differences in dogs and for diverse personalities (dogs and owners) and for individual lifestyles.

A word of warning, however. Don't fall into the "I've tried everything" trap! When several possible solutions are offered, it does not mean you should flit from one to another. Quite the reverse. Decide first which method most closely fits your situation. Then stick with it. When there's a behavior problem, it can take weeks before your chosen solution works. (The bad habit didn't happen overnight either.) Trying "everything" will result in a confused dog that doesn't know what you want and will pick and choose what suits him or her, convincing you the method is not working. It's the same as the warning that constantly changing dog foods will land you with a finicky eater who wants to see the whole menu and be allowed substitutions! *Dogs thrive on consistency*.

A good part of the trust that's essential between you and your dog is built on your predictability. Rufus uses all your various actions, from the obvious (picking up the car keys that means you're leaving) to the minimal (the "evil eye" that means no). It is this predictable consistency that develops trust. That is why parenting and discipline must be predictable. Both dogs and toddlers rely on it. It's the kind of trust that's reinforced by holding a parent's hand, or going for a walk on-leash.

Therefore, in using toddler training theories and methods, you may be surprised how many can be applied to dogs while still treating the dog as a dog. I'm convinced that dogs kept as pets can be likened to our children without resorting to anthropomorphizing. A dog is always a more satisfactory pet when accepted for "dogginess" rather than for childlike attributes. Some of the differences I would hope are pretty obvious, but it is hard not to make certain comparisons when a dog becomes part of our family. There's even a bumper sticker that says, "The more I learn about mankind, the more I love my dog." Many versions of the sentiment abound, so the general concept is a popular one.

WHEN PARENTING BEGINS

Learning about canine parenting begins when you first decide you'd like to add a dog to the household, regardless of whether you are thinking about puppy or adult, large breed or small, purebred or mixed. The choices are purely personal, many owners confess to their decision having been based purely on the dog's looks! But being practical, the size should fit your living space, both the temperament and the athletic capability need to match yours and the age of the dog should hinge to a great extent upon your work schedule.

Come to a firm agreement with everyone in the household as to these specifics (including physical attributes), or else hidden resentment could surface every time the dog does anything wrong. You know . . . "The *Beagle* I wanted wouldn't have dug up the backyard." "A *Cocker Spaniel* wouldn't have spilled the water!" "If we'd gotten a *Collie*, it would be *fun* to walk the dog."

A major reason puppies and their conscientious new owners run into problems later on is that they get off to a bad start on day one. They invariably receive some or all the necessary "parenting" information at the precise moment they pick up their puppy. Given the dilemma of being charmed by an adorable warm puppy licking your face or absorbing instructions (which may seem to be in a foreign language), it's no wonder so many never even hear the part that says, in effect, "Batteries not included."

Well ahead of puppy pickup time, puppy sellers would do well to provide buyers with all the how-tos pertinent to that breed, a list of essentials (crate, collar, leash, dishes, toys, grooming tools, food) and this book for a better understanding of problem prevention.

Given a couple of weeks to familiarize themselves with most of the information, and with some of the little things (like how to open and close the crate door), the owners can relax and enjoy those *vital* first forty-eight hours when the puppy bounces in upon the scene. The equipment is at hand, the family knows how to use it and has decided where to put it. It pays to be prepared. And I know what you're thinking. Yes indeed, this IS just like bringing home the baby!

A young puppy left alone all day will learn how to do everything you do NOT want it to do, and will be deprived of what every dog needs most—company. Puppies are excellent students, but they make lousy teachers! Forget the worn-out myths about old dogs. They certainly can learn new tricks, new lifestyles and bond to a new family. If dogs had not learned to go with the flow when they were put on earth, they wouldn't be around today.

One possible cause for failure in dog ownership, particularly in the case of a working family, is when the dog is put in the same position as the TV wife of the 1950s. "Stay home, mind the house and don't do anything creative while I'm gone." Dogs are intelligent enough not to take kindly to this form of canine chauvinism! They become bored and stressed, and unlike those long-suffering wives, dogs take their feelings out on their environment by destroying couches, demolishing table legs, digging holes in walls or floors and generally being *exceptionally* creative. Dogs have a far better chance at making it on the family team when parented like the toddler but accepted above all for being exactly what they are: dogs.

THE SINGLE "PARENT"

Lifestyles do change, and they have as great an effect (good or bad) on the dog as on the people involved. The real single parent has only fairly recently gained social acceptance in this country, but the single "parent" of a dog is not only accepted on every social level, it is also a perfect partnership. It is even fully endorsed by the medical profession, because owning a dog provides the solo person with non-critical companionship, a warm feeling of being wanted and needed, and also gives a good reason for exercise. The dog agrees with every-thing we say, and gives the kind of greeting at the end of a day that's motivation enough to go home after work.

So you say these are some of the reasons you want to share your life with your dog and that's great. But sharing is a fifty-fifty proposition, and if you've allowed dear Rufus to encroach on your half beyond what are acceptable limits, he will suffer the effects of exces-sive attention. His canine identity will be lost, and since he isn't capable of filling the role of a human child, poor Rufus is in limbo. Ignoring won't be easy, but stick to shunning *some* of his wheedling ways, and once you're doing well with this weaning process, begin to introduce outside attention—from friends, strangers, other dogs. So that people won't think you're accosting them on the street, sign up for an Obedi-ence class for socialization and to teach your—oh, let's say it—your spoiled dog-child how to enjoy being a dog.

Obedience Training—What It Teaches

Obedience training is not meant to solve behavioral problems. But it is an excellent place to start because it provides you with the necessary tools for good communication. The training puts the dog's

Single "parent" of a dog feels wanted and needed.

8

Obedience training gives you the tools—but it's hard to show Basil Basset how to sit!

owner-parent into a parenting role if only by providing you with reliable safety signals. In this respect, a dog is a whole lot easier to teach than a young child. Drop a bottle of medicine on the floor, and one "Leave it!" followed by a Sit-Stay, and you can pick up every pill. A toddler might, or might not, react as dependably.

Parenting is not something you "do" on weekends or the way you might "do lunch." It is a sedulous activity. You send a youngster off to school and breathe a sigh of relief knowing someone else will have the "parenting" (as well as tutorial) job for a few hours, but not so with the dog.

You go to school, too, in order to understand how a dog learns. Child educators figure most parents have some idea of how schools operate, although the parallels are there: Parents who don't, have a tougher job being a parent!

Dogs don't learn from lectures (except to reach for the OFF button) and they don't learn from constantly hearing "No!" If Obedience training does nothing else for the owner, it does explain that the quickest way to teach a dog is via the Missouri method. You know: "Show me!"

THE FEAR FACTOR

Dr. Alvin N. Eden, in *Positive Parenting*, states: "Somewhere between four and six months of age, some babies develop a fear of strangers. This can be considered normal behavior." And what do all the experts on the growing puppy tell us? That between four and six months puppies go through a "fear period" and that it is normal. Pup and baby are parented in much the same ways through this stage.

Verbal language used to be considered the primary difference in approach, but now infant psychologists find that babies (like puppies) do indeed read our body language, sense our emotions. A dog is just a quicker study. Don't force the situation. Remain your cheery-voiced, confident self if your outgoing, friendly pup suddenly turns into a scaredy-cat. Let the pup hide first and come out to make friends on its own terms. It wouldn't hurt to fortify said friends with a couple of treats to be offered *after* the pup has made overtures.

The best thing about this fear phase is that it is soon history. It occurs in all breeds, but not in all individual dogs. Some pups exhibit fearful behavior for a couple of days, some for a month, therefore this should not be confused with either shyness or a truly fearful dog. The shy pup was, is and probably always will be shy. A fearful dog generally will show its true colors by biting when between six and twelve months of age.

Reducing Fear

A baby can be physically comforted. Not so the puppy. Don't use force. Don't pick up the pup. Don't say comforting things like, "It's okay, Dinkums," because it is definitely *not* okay, just normal. The sooner Dinkums gets over it, the better for everyone. Take consolation in the fact that the phase will end as the canine version of social security emerges.

An adult dog that persists in fearful behavior (no longer just somewhat shy) has an emotional problem that needs professional help. Such dogs may become what are called "fear biters." They behave in a fearful manner, often hiding behind their owner, then attack with the speed of lightning and instantly retreat to safety behind their owner.

This is definitely not the dog to have around children. But the excuse given is often the same as for the genuinely timid dog—"Puffy is fine once she gets to know you. She's just afraid of strangers." Words of warning! Shyness and fearfulness are not the same thing.

SHY DOG, SHY CHILD

Shyness is a temperament that may be genetic, or it may be environmentally induced. We saw that the fear phase comes as a surprise in an otherwise friendly, outgoing dog and is a sudden but temporary reaction to certain strange, new things. Shyness is a personality type that lacks self-confidence. It is constant, and shows none of the frantic signs of a fearful dog. Shyness is generally less noticeable at home where the dog may even at times give the appearance of getting over it. This seldom happens.

There are no similar statistics on dogs, but about one in five babies is said to be born with a tendency toward shyness. Given time and thoughtful consideration, rather than pushing, most kids outgrow it. (Those that don't may become comedians or actors—Johnny Carson, Sir Lawrence Olivier!)

A shy dog will not outgrow this attitude all by itself, primarily because pet dogs remain pre-adolescent. A breeder can begin parenting the shy pup with gentle extra handling, taking it away from the litter with the next-quietest pup for one-on-one canine interaction, etc. The new owner takes it from there, never forcing the pup into uncomfortable situations, but instead calmly encouraging it to investigate at the dogs own pace, with quiet verbal praise for any success.

Keep in mind that shyness in any animal is part of a need for self-preservation. You'll hear similar statements over and over again to remind you this book *is* about parenting dogs, not kids! Self-preservation is a primary concern to a dog. It would be foolhardy for a dog to bounce up to every single thing without some degree of caution. The shy pup was just born with a little more caution in makeup than some littermates.

The shy dog still has a place in the scheme of things. The truly shy dog that does not gain self-confidence, most likely has an owner

For some kids or adults a somewhat shy dog is a perfect choice.

who finds shyness to be a charming trait and has no desire to change it. (But don't hold your breath. The shy dog will simply remain delightfully shy. It won't become a star of stage or screen!)

A timid dog makes a great pet for an elderly person, or for anyone of any age whose lifestyle is low key or solitary. Shyness can be a bonus trait for someone who would be overwhelmed by a more effusive, demanding dog. A truly shy dog is not a threat to anyone, and with the right owner can be tolerated as is, or even better, can have confidence boosted to a point where much of the shyness is overcome.

No one should be put off acquiring a shy pup by being told that all shy dogs are fear biters. Many dog trainers have taken to lumping all shy and fearful dogs together (including pups in the fear phase) and calling them fear biters, which is like saying all outgoing dogs are aggressive attack dogs. With good parenting practices, there's room for a broad range of acceptable individualism in our pets in general as well as within specific breeds.

If you have a fully grown dog with temperament problems that include biting, it doesn't much matter if the diagnosis is fear biter, shy-aggressive, dominant-aggressive or is given any other name. You need an expert's help. A bite isn't less painful or less dangerous because you attach a label to it.

Carol was told by all her friends to pick the most outgoing pup in the litter, but when she looked at the four adorable Maltese puppies, the one that caught her eye and her heart was the one that sat in the corner of the pen, sizing her up while the others vied for attention. The breeder called the pup a shrinking violet. Two years later, Violet (what else?) is a perfect companion. She still views strangers carefully (so does Carol) but she offers a quiet well-mannered welcome to friends who come to the house. For eight months Violet avoided all other dogs, but now has a crush on a very large chocolate Labrador and has completely accepted a kitten companion. Carol couldn't be happier with her choice.

Friends and strangers can be a problem for the shy dog and its owner. They want to pet the dog, talk to it, etc., and the shy dog really needs to be totally ignored until such time as it gathers enough courage to make overtures. Ask friends to visit, sit down and pay NO attention to the dog, while you remain in control, saying a quiet rewarding "Good dog" for every small attempt the dog makes to bridge the gap.

Say *nothing*, nothing at all, to the dog while it continues to be withdrawn. Whatever you might say (remember the language barrier) will be mistaken by the dog for approval. The last thing you want to do is promote shyness. This is not the pup to socialize via crowds, noise or other confusion, but then, for the low-key owner, it is the perfect companion for TV watching or sitting in front of a fire with a good book.

BRAG TIME

Parents can get into prickly situations when comparing notes with other parents. Johnny hasn't yet mastered the use of a spoon and same-age Arlene is using a knife and fork! Marcy is putting barrettes in her hair and Derek can't match two shoes! On and on it goes—the brag list, with pride on the up side, and with guilt or depression on the down side.

You're wrong if you think it's different with dogs; and they don't fare any better in these comparison tests. The minute you brag that Tootsie was housebroken in four weeks, you hear that Trixie accomplished it in two, or you say that Rambo graduated first in pre-novice Obedience, you are told that Leroy already has AKC Obedience titles.

Next time the brags come at you, and you don't feel like playing the game, be ready with a stopper: "All dogs are so smart! And all so different." The smile on your face might be mistaken for licking cream, but no one can argue with what you've said.

BONDING

The bonding of a baby with its two parents is a relatively new field of study, and the bonding of dogs and their primary caregivers is now recognized as an essential ingredient for success in the development of trusting, good relationships with other people, too. The dog that bonds well trusts others.

Bonding plays a particularly important part in the adoption of an

Some shy dogs may turn to the stage!

older dog regardless of where it came from—a shelter, breeder, college son or the death of Aunt Em. Use the umbilical cord method. Put the dog on a long soft leash attached to a buckle collar and tie the other end to your belt or waist. The point of this exercise is to keep Rufus literally with you for every waking hour. (Well, not quite. The bathroom is yours alone.)

In the course of two or three days Rufus will learn all kinds of little things he needs to know about you. How you move, speak, smell, react to the doorbell, to the telephone and household appliances, what you eat and when you eat it. Where the dog's own place is during meals. Which doors you use for what—oh, the list is endless, but the dog will learn it all quickly and without making any mistakes, because you're there to prevent them.

You will be learning what your dog's reactions are to all these things, plus when Rufus needs to go out, what words he may already know, what things are upsetting (although you may never know why), what things you do that are particularly pleasing.

Any significant other in the household can go through the bonding process, too. This is not an exclusive club, although I would not recommend it for children because it is too restrictive and, let's be honest, b-o-r-i-n-g!

As with the baby, the bonding process for the dog begins as soon as the dog arrives, not after it has established its own version of the rules and the pack order. The most important side effect of bonding is the establishment of trust.

TRUST

Trust is another prime ingredient in raising both a baby and a dog. However, the methods for developing it differ somewhat because a baby's and a dog's needs proceed at different rates. A dog wants you to be consistent in such things as rules, safety, food, handling and play from day one.

Trust can go awry from something as simple as a puppy being teased. Teasing actually teaches a dog that you cannot be trusted because your actions are not predictable. This distrust can then expand to include all men, or all women, or all kids. On the other hand, an adult dog that has learned to trust will accept good-natured teasing recognized as play, because he *does* trust and can read playful intentions.

BACK TALK

Children talk back. We may not like it and may heartily disapprove of it. In public we probably find it singularly embarrassing. But they do it because it is normal and healthy. From the toddler's first "No!" to the teenager's "Make me!" children need to test the boundaries to find out how far they can go. Being sassy is also one more way to get attention when the limits are not clearly defined.

Dogs use the same scenario. There are two distinct phases when barking back is apt to be tried out. When three or four months of age, the puppy will often bark in response to your telling the dog to do something it already knows or is learning how to do. Our reaction

Basil Basset still can't sit straight but is being told barking back won't help his cause.

tends to be the same as that of the toddler's parent—amusement. Baby is growing up. How cute. As anyone who's been there can tell you, it soon wears thin and the cute "no" turns into the "terrible twos" and the bark back becomes "nuisance barking."

Treat barking seriously. The young pup needs to have you follow through on whatever you told the dog to do. Stay good-natured and friendly, *teach, don't punish*, but don't take the pup's "no" for an answer. If the barking continues, and interferes with what you were doing (say, teaching the pup to accept a collar and leash), then hold a hand firmly over the dog's muzzle or give one sharp tap on top of the muzzle AS you say "NO bark!" Obviously, the barking has to stop even for a millisecond.

Add a "Good dog" and continue the lesson. (This is one of the times when the rules for handling a toddler/puppy situation differ.) The next time you'll run into barking is when the pup at around ten months becomes a canine teenager. This is the challenge bark of "Make me." And that's exactly what you will do—firmly, but with good humor, distractions and a food reward for compliance.

As you see, the back talk (or bark back) from a dog does not carry over into social rudeness, but it is a tool for negotiating and is part of growing up. It is every bit as normal and natural for a dog to chew, bite, bark or have an occasional accident as it is for a baby to spit up, coo and soil its diapers. But with a dog you have Mother Nature on your side: The dog's life cycle is speeded up so it becomes as much an adult as it ever will be in just two short years. Whew!

GOOD DOG

Here is another parenting principle that works with dogs, yet few people use it to their advantage. Catch your dog doing something RIGHT and reinforce it by using the word the dog has learned to associate with that action, combined with praise. For example, Rufus is lying down, not asleep, just lying there watching the world go by. Say "Good DOWN." Rufus is sitting watching you scrape carrots. You know, and I know, and Rufus knows, that he's waiting for a piece to drop fortuitously to the floor. Instead, praise with "Good SIT" and a smile.

SEPARATION

There are many traumatic moments experienced by good dog owners (good parents) as their pups (offspring) grow up. One is separation anxiety. It's that awful feeling when your toddler first goes off to nursery school. You're proud as punch—and terrified. So is your child. Or when the older child wants to sleep over at a friend's house—and calls you at 10:30 P.M. to come get him. The cool, calm way in which you handle all these attempts to leave the nest will help to build the child's self-confidence.

Sleeping away from home is sometimes so traumatic for a child that the parents decide to forego vacations. For the youngster, there is the apprehension of a strange bed, strange room, combined with separation anxiety (no Mommy, no Daddy). And yes, the very same thing can happen when the dog is put into a boarding kennel. Much of this can be avoided if you are smart and train your dog to *enjoy* a crate (Chapter 6).

You won't hear, "I want my Mommy!" but you may get the canine version, the barking, whining, drooling even before you get to the kennel. For the dog that walks into the kennel on all fours, there is something known as the sudden brake syndrome. Anti-lock or not, the dog appears frozen in time and space and will not move one inch further voluntarily.

Of course, this is where you would repeat to Lucy what you've been telling her for days, "Daddy and I will call you tonight from Bermuda, and if you're a good girl Grandma will let you bake cookies . . . ." What you say to the dog is, with a big smiley face and cheerful voice, "What a good Rufus" *as* you hand over the leash to the kennel staff.

Rufus will soon be satisfying his curiosity about the new surroundings, new people and new canine friends (or foes). Just as you don't keep telling a child how much you'll miss her in order not to build up more anxiety than already exists, so you shouldn't say anything more than that quick, happy-sounding goodbye to Rufus. Use the same smile-goodbye-and-go principle when you leave the house, or drop Rufus off at the groomer's. The dog grasps your feelings and emotions, not your explanations.

Other Separations

Other, bigger separations cause anxiety, like divorce or Mom returning to the work force, which are fully covered in Chapter 10.

These things are part of life. Some take a lot of planning, whether a dog or a youngster is involved. There's no need to feel guilty about it. Feelings of guilt can have two adverse effects on your dog. Either Rufus will become increasingly spoiled by your unwarranted attention to compensate for leaving, or he will experience excessive stress from picking up on your strained emotions.

So, unless you're a glutton for self-punishment (and lack consideration for your dog), throw guilt and its negative effects out the window.

Parents who have not learned how "to parent" correctly, and who therefore cannot properly administer discipline, often feel guilty. True with kids. True with dogs. Chuck the guilt. Besides, you won't need it. The next chapter is all about discipline.

For further reading

Spoiled Rotten, by Fred Gossman (Villard Books, NY 1992)
Perfect Parenting and Other Myths, by Frank Main, Ed.D. (Comp Care Publications, MN 1992)

2

The Disciplines

A DEFINITION

Dictionaries are remarkably in agreement over the meaning of the word *discipline*, using such phrases as, ". . . rigorous training of the mental, moral and physical powers by instruction and exercise. The result of this. Self-control."* Or, "Training . . . to produce a specific character or pattern of behavior."**

Note the use of "rigorous," "exercise" and "self-control," all things we would use in training our dogs. If discipline (or training) is namby-pamby rather than rigorous, we can expect wishy-washy results. Similarly, we know that proper exercise is good not only for the body, but also for the mental stimulus it provides.

The goal of our disciplining is to have a dog with self-control, one that will walk down the street paying little or no attention to a barking or growling dog behind the fence, a dog that will sit still and

*The Doubleday Dictionary
**The American Heritage Dictionary

The goal is a dog that will tolerate the adoration of children, a dog we can trust.

tolerate the adoration of young children; in other words, a dog we can trust. When discipline is lacking, the same dog would take on the barker behind the fence, and with unrestrained exhuberance would bounce among the kids, probably knocking them down in the process.

In these examples, the dog is not obeying or disobeying Obedience commands, but is exhibiting self-control or the lack of it. This is disciplined behavior or its absence.

The Oxford Universal Dictionary offers the definition that comes closest to what this book is all about: "Instruction imparted to disciples or scholars; teaching; learning; education."

Correctly understood and used, as you will see, discipline is a preventive measure and, therefore, precludes the need for punishment. Having been disciplined (or taught) what is right, the dog will continue trying to win your ongoing approval. Note that *"discipline" means both teaching and learning*, which we can redefine for our purposes to mean that you cannot teach a dog without learning something yourself.

WHAT WORKS, WHAT DOESN'T

There are certain strategies involved in disciplining that simply do not work with children and are just as bad or worse when used with dogs. They are common reactions to our own failure in preventing the problem in the first place. Here are some of the worst-case scenarios— all very widespread human failings!

YELLING: Yelling or shouting at a dog is a complete waste of time and energy. The dog may cower at the anger in your voice, but that look on the dog's face is not guilt, shame or sorrow, no matter how much most dog owners like to think it is. It is submission or fear, if yelling is normally followed by physical abuse, and the dog is showing you that yielding to your higher authority is the best way to get you to stop the outburst.

Like children, dogs eventually build up an immunity to your noise and find innovative ways to tune you out. Brucie, an Airedale, was so tuned in to family arguments over finances that if he saw anyone pick up the checkbook, he'd retreat in a head-first dive between the sheets of the youngest child's bed!

PHYSICAL ABUSE: This is a sure sign the owner has lost it. Good parenting and good discipline do not include abuse. Hitting a dog with a rolled-up newspaper, your hand or with anything else only teaches the dog one thing: to stay out of arm's reach. Physical abuse is severe punishment, not discipline, and can easily backfire, turning even a docile dog into an unmanageable and aggressive one. It has no re-deeming feature.

There are forms of physical correction, such as the "shake" or "pinning," which dogs do understand, but these are used in specific ways and in precise situations, never abusively. Suffice it to say, physical abuse does not work.

FORCE: This is similar to physical abuse, but may not be done in anger and is not intended to be cruel. An example of the use of force with good intentions would be putting a pinch or prong collar on a puppy to teach the Sit. It's overkill. Dragging a puppy along by the collar and leash before it has learned to accept these devices is also using unnecessary force, as is trying to shove a puppy into a crate.

A Good Motto: Teach, don't traumatize.

NAGGING: This is another waste of time and effort on kids and dogs, since both will soon stop listening. A classic example is the owner who says, "Sit, Rufus. Sit. Sit! Rufus SIT! RUFUS! SIT!" The only way to teach the dog is to say the word once and immediately show the dog the desired action. Dogs are not linguists, so all they get from nagging is "blah, blah, blah" with an occasional word they recognize—such as their name. There's an old Scottish saying that applies to both yelling and nagging, "Save your breath to cool your porridge." Enough said?

ANGER: The dog is the butt of the family's anger more often than we care to admit, primarily because the dog is at the bottom of the family's social scale. Anger thrives on a chain reaction. Dad is mad at Mom, so Mom takes out her discontent on an older child. He turns on his young sister and she, having no one else to pull rank on, takes her frustration out on the dog. (There is another side to this which we'll get to later.)

The sliding of anger down to the lowest one on the totem pole, in this case the dog, is another reason why toddlers do not make good dog owners. In mimicking adult anger, the toddler may overreact, taking it out on the family pet and get hurt as a result. Not every Rufus can accept such unwarranted human behavior, especially because Rufus may consider the toddler to be a littermate (or less) and so cope with the outburst in a normal dog fashion. (That is, with teeth, if you didn't already know!)

Beyond an angry facial expression of disapproval when the dog is caught in the act of misbehaving (and only then, not a minute later), skip anger. Unless you can come up with a great imitation of a growl, your anger will not translate into anything the dog can understand. Take Archie Bunker's advice, "Stifle it!"

24

SHAME: Parents are warned not to shame a child because it lowers self-esteem and does more harm than good. Trainers sometimes use the word *shame* when the dog has not correctly obeyed a command, but any other word would do the job as well. The intent is to stop an inappropriate behavior in order to teach the correct one. ("AACHT" works better.) Attempts to shame a dog include such totally meaningless things as "shoving his nose in it," or tying a forbidden object on the dog's collar. (I've heard of everything from sneakers to garbage.) It doesn't work. Shame is connected to conscience, and dogs don't have one.

GUILT: Guilt is something you can lay on a child (not advisable or admirable, but it is possible). However, so far as we know, dogs do not have feelings of guilt because they do not take responsibility for their mistakes. This may be attributed to the juvenile mentality of the dog, or more likely, to the fact that we have developed a conscience and animals have not. Whatever the precise explanation, it is important to accept the concept in order to read your dog's body language correctly.

That "guilty look" every dog owner thinks he or she sees many times in the dog's life is NOT guilt. What elicits that hang-dog expression is the dog's way of avoiding your outburst or of showing submission to your superiority. Either way, if it stops you in your tracks, the dog figures it's the right response.

Let's say you arrive home from work to a scene of utter destruction and you are scolding (yelling, shouting, gesticulating—oh, I do hope you aren't, but maybe it was a hard day at the office), and the dog, appropriately for a dog, responds to your antics with "that look." That look is submission. If a pup could say "uncle" (just to get you to stop) he would, but that is precisely what that look is trying to convey. A dog would never say the words we want to hear, "I'm sorry, I'll never ever do it again," so we put them into the dog's mouth, add a mournful face and call the whole package "guilt."

Let's put a positive light on it. The dog puts on a submissive face (and no doubt the body follows, with everything lowered—head, ears, tail between the legs) to show you in the only way he can that you are the acknowledged leader, Top Dog, Best Friend. Rufus can't clean up the mess or mend the carpet, and the mere thought of it would never occur to your dog. Of this whole scenario, the important point to keep in mind is *The dog only connects your anger with what was being done when you opened the door*. Maybe sleeping? Greeting you? What both you and the dog need is a cooling-off period. Now is the perfect moment for a Time-Out.

THE POSITIVE APPROACH

If you are right there when the dog is about to make a mistake of any kind, let out a nasty, gutteral "AACHT!" to show that what your pup has in mind is a no-no (for example, *about* to steal your snack, or just *eyeing* your T-shirt on the floor). Catch Rufus in the act of leaping onto the couch or grabbing the T-shirt, and get in your "NO! BAD DOG!" promptly. Separate dog from the forbidden object and say no more.

Nagging, yelling, anger, physical force, remember, do not work because they are all negative approaches that will indeed produce reactions from the dog—negative ones. *Discipline is a positive teaching device.* You cannot teach or "parent" or discipline just by saying no all the time. That doesn't work with a child and it doesn't work with a dog. But because of the language barrier, it is even more important that the dog be taught what is right, what has your approval, what is acceptable and what you want instead of dwelling on "No! Bad dog." Lots of the rules are the same, but keep in mind that this is a dog, not a child, you're "parenting."

Attention becomes a reward to a dog, or a child, regardless of whether it is positive or negative in form. It's easy to fall into the trap of scolding a pup, only to have the dog repeat the misbehavior, so you scold again. And the scenario is repeated. The dog is luxuriating in all the attention—even though it is negative and even though you may think you are punishing the dog. This is not a healthy situation.

Punishment, to be good discipline, must be firm enough to stop the unwanted behavior entirely. Think of attention as a reward, sometimes earned and sometimes spontaneous, but always positive.

"AACHT!" Don't even THINK about stealing it!

Now we come to something that, while a negative for children, is a very positive measure for teaching our canine friends.

Setting a Trap

Entrapment is not at all an acceptable thing to do to a child because it has moral overtones. It would be wrong, for example, to set up a child to be forced to tell a lie—and then to dole out punishment for lying.

However, setting a trap for a dog in order to eliminate the unwanted behavior puts the owner in a position to teach an acceptable alternative, and works well because it simplifies and speeds up the entire lesson.

A correction is only fully understood by the dog if that correction takes place precisely *as* the dog is misbehaving. For example, your dog tips over the kitchen trash can. You discover it sometime later and know you mustn't punish for a past action. You could sit home for hours waiting for the dog to get the urge (or the courage) to do it again. Loads of dogs are smart enough not to go near a forbidden object when you're home. Eating upset garbage or overturning wastepaper baskets are bored-dog activities. It makes more sense for you to get the lesson over with and do something that's more fun.

There are several ways to ambush a naughty dog. If you cannot be home, one way is to use a device I call a Stop-It can (see footnote on page 96). An Afghan Hound that had figured out how to step on the pedal and silently open the garbage can, was retrained by tying one Stop-It can inside the lid and casually leaving another on top. Instead of garbage goodies, the dog got a loud *CRASH* from two directions. The noise is enough to deter most dogs from testing it a second time. This method sets the dog up, but provides an unpleasant association when you're not around to do it.

Another way to use entrapment is to leave a bit of food (a slice or two of hot dog is irresistible) on top of the trash can and lie in wait for the canine thief. This, however, definitely requires your presence. Far enough removed to give the culprit the green light, but close enough to make the all-important disclaimer.

When you're around and you see Spot (Rufus would never!) about

Caught in the act of the trash can caper.

to sniff or investigate, use "AACHT" in place of "No" because the dog has not actually done anything wrong—yet! It's one of those don't-even-think-it situations that is better served by a warning than a correction.

Some dogs can't tolerate the sound or taste of aluminum foil, in which case a bouffant skirt of foil around the top of trash cans, wastepaper baskets or houseplants will turn away the would-be felon. Others only lick the edges of these containers, which, of course, can fortuitously result in tipping them over!

Applying a substance such as Grannick's Bitter Apple, or Tabasco pepper sauce to the edges may do the trick. These two suggestions are self-correcting, so you don't necessarily have to hang around. I say "necessarily" from experience, however. One little dog in my house developed a passion for Tabasco pepper sauce, Bitter Apple, lemon juice, cayenne pepper and chili peppers! There's no accounting for taste. Some people swear by the water pistol correction, but some dogs think it's play not punishment, and it's messy to say the least. All of which shows us once again that there is no *one* right way to discipline all dogs.

This Instant!

Your dog with a Utility Degree (or child with a Ph.D.) will usually give you instant action on command, but expecting an average puppy or youngster to give you immediate compliance is just plain unrealistic. (And note that I tempered the first sentence with "usually." "Always" is also unrealistic!)

Often the request is combined with the wrong situation. For example, you discover a corner of the bedroom rug has been "redesigned" (chewed, soaked or otherwise destroyed). The order goes out loud and clear: "Spot! Come here! Come here this instant! Look what you did! What did you do?"

No puppy or older dog (or child) would fail to hear the anger in your voice and know immediately that it would be a far, far wiser thing NOT to come anywhere near you!

Golden Rule: NEVER call a dog to come to you to receive a punishment, and NEVER punish a "bad" dog when it does come to you. This is a 100 percent written-in-stone rule. Remember it when the dog has run away from you and finally returns, or you get within calling distance after a two-mile road race. There are *no* exceptions to this rule.

While we're on this subject, there are two primary reasons why a dog refuses to come when called. One, as we've discussed, is because it was told to "come" in order to be punished. The other is because it was called when off-lead and was therefore allowed the luxury of exercising a choice: to come, or not to come—that is the question, and the answer from the dog is "a definite maybe." Believe me, the dog will learn these two things more quickly than any of the things you work hard to teach.

So, once again: Unless you catch Rufus in the act, forget the punishment. Give your dog and yourself a Time-Out to think about how you can prevent it from happening again.

The Big "Yeah, But . . ."

Let's get real. The dog destroyed the couch while you were out and knowing *now* that the dog should have been confined is not going to mend the couch or soothe your anger. In this case we are dealing not only with the dog and what the dog has done, but with your understandable and very human fury about something over which you *had* no control. Now you do have control.

The answer is a Time-Out. Only a professional upholsterer will be able to fix the couch. Only by giving yourself some space will you be able to get rid of your anger and frustration. Only by putting the dog somewhere safe (confined and preferably out of earshot of your ravings) will you be able to come to grips with the situation in a reasonable way. If your favorite place for a Time-Out is under the shower, you are not alone. Many a tear has gone down many a drain for less.

Terry told me her dog, Mickey, kept "paddling" on the seat of the armchair or couch. The dog was really digging, or nesting. (Mickey was obviously not a very large dog or the couch and chair would be in shreds! Mickey, it turns out, is a Pomeranian.) Almost every dog performs this nesting ritual, some more than others. Some dig, some just turn around and around. Some do both. Every dog owner should know that this is as normal and natural to a dog as scratching an itch with a hind leg. It is one reason to keep dogs off furniture.

Terry had thought Mickey was a canine mental case and therefore never mentioned it to anyone. She was relieved to hear it was normal behavior. As to how long this had bothered her? Five years! Her "yeah, but" was that she liked having the little dog next to her on the couch, so she never stopped him from being there. When she was around to witness the "paddling" she just picked him up, gave him a cuddle and put him back on the couch! She was, in effect, praising the dog for wrecking the couch.

Here's a similar problem but with a large dog. In three months, a one-year-old Irish Setter had chewed up three living room chairs, four patio cushions and three azalea bushes, among numerous other things. The dog was left outside while its owners went to work, but was "free" in the house if they went shopping or to the movies. Add to this the fact that the husband "did not believe in" Obedience training, only *corporal punishment*. The wife was getting nowhere trying to teach the dog what little she knew about Obedience.

What a mess! And this is not an isolated case; similar canine predicaments occur in thousands of dogs' homes everywhere. It's a classic case of a dog being frustrated by inconsistency, mixed mes-

Some people put up with things like begging, sitting on the couch. To each her own.

sages, a lack of discipline and not being taught what's right. It had become a life of constant punishment—everything the dog did was wrong.

It took lots of convincing, but the husband agreed to try the idea of replacing punishment with a Time-Out. There are apt to be many days when a pup's behavior goes from bad to worse, so the owners were cautioned to call a Time-Out right after *bad*, and definitely before *worse*. Irish was introduced to a crate and took to it happily for her owners' trips to the mall, market or movies. Teaching the dog by approval brought about a big change in the dog's behavior.

The wife decided to give Obedience classes a try and guess who changed his mind when he saw the results? Last I heard Irish is "a pretty good dog now, but she was a terrible puppy." All three members of the family seem to have settled their differences.

Punishment

In child studies conducted independently all over the country, psychologists reached similar conclusions regarding the effects of physical punishment. Children who are routinely spanked for misbehavior tend to be less obedient and more likely to be depressed. Dr. Irwin A. Hyman of Temple University in Philadelphia goes so far as to say, "All the evidence suggests that frequent spanking is more likely the cause, not the result, of disobedience and mental illness."

He then offers this further explanation, which has direct application to puppies. "The problem starts early with parents who fail to understand normal child development and spank infants and toddlers when they act naturally, for example, when they grab things off a table." This is exactly the type of thing I hear from puppy owners.

Hitting does not work because it doesn't offer the dog an acceptable alternative way to behave. Bob said his five-month old German Shepherd Dog ate the crackers and cheese he had put out for guests, but when Bob whacked the pup for it, the pup bit him.

Unfortunately, it is the kind of response you can expect from a puppy that's been "whacked." Leaving a puppy alone with accessible, desirable food is asking for trouble. This is a good time for that rolled-up newspaper so many dog owners want to use. But use it to whack

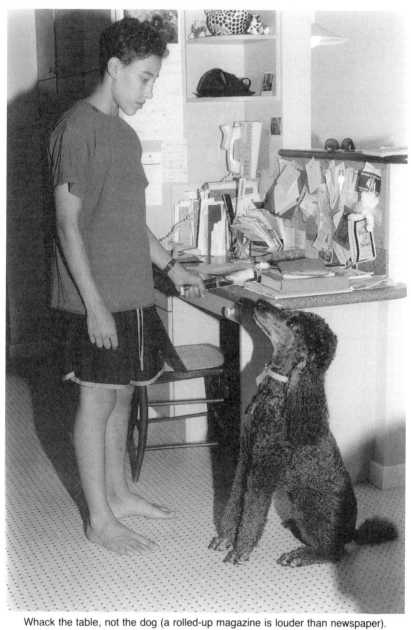

Whack the table, not the dog (a rolled-up magazine is louder than newspaper).

the table, or a wall or your leg—*not the dog.* (A magazine delivers a far better crack than newspaper.) Again, this is a case of catching the dog in the act, giving a sharp noise distraction as you say "NO!" When the pup knows right from wrong, but tests you, use "AACHT!"

There is something that *can* happen as a result of physical correction. Like toddlers who are victims of abuse, dogs that are hit or hung by a choke chain to "teach 'em a lesson," for example, or in any way abused, are at high risk to become excessively aggressive by the time they become "teenagers," a phase that kicks in at about ten months of age in dogs and is normally very short-lived.

Owners invariably believe the changes came on suddenly, "yesterday an angel, today a monster." The true teenage syndrome— testing your rules, trying your patience, behaving like an adult one minute and a little puppy the next—does come on quickly and leaves the same way, thank goodness, often in a matter of days.

But in the case of behavioral problems caused by physical abuse, the owner is dealing with a serious matter. Success will depend in part on the specific breed of dog, how long the mistreatment has gone on and the owner's ability to implement the changes necessary to exercise discipline by teaching rather than by physical counterattack. The cure does not come in a book. Seek qualified professional help immediately.

Discipline puts a limit on the dog's behavior and molds it into what is acceptable for your lifestyle, but it does not and should not squelch the dog's personality or attitude, nor spoil its natural temperament. Discipline will not turn a Collie into a Scottie.

Dr. Katherine Houpt of Cornell University bases a need for owners to be wary of severe physical punishment on another, clinical, reason. In tests on dogs and cats, it was found that when pups, for example, knew the end result would be unpleasant, they totally tuned out the exercise. The phenomenon is given the name "learned helplessness." Perhaps this, too, goes all the way back to the basics of self-preservation. No matter the origin, beware that the "stubbornness" sometimes referred to by trainers may actually be caused by abusive training methods and therefore is not stubbornness at all, but learned helplessness.

Before attempting to discipline your dog for misbehavior, determine what actually triggers it. Dogs react to specific sounds or sights. For example:

- Is the doorbell a signal for a fit of barking? It's normal. Teach tolerance by "saturation," i.e., relentless repetition of doorbell ringing.
- Does the sound of the toaster bring on instant begging? Normal, if you have *ever* shared a crunchy piece of toast.
- Do people in hats or sunglasses, kids with toys or some other sight bring on unseemly behavior? Normal, if your dog has not been thoroughly socialized to accept a variety of strangers.
- Does nipping begin when the kids' playtime gets rowdy? Normal, but a Time-Out is indicated—for the kids, too.

Some behavior problems in dogs begin, and then escalate, because of the completely normal reactions of their owners. If you panic when the doorbell rings, so will your dog. If you hand out treats all morning, your dog will beg all afternoon and night!

In using *praise* as a reward for good behavior, here are some guidelines to follow.

1. If you've been trying to teach one thing for six weeks and Bozo finally catches on, be lavish with your praise—big smiles, happy voice, even a brief body rub.
2. Calm down and repeat the performance, and if Bozo gets it right *this* time, use more rational praise.
3. A smile and "Good dog" will do. Bribery is okay, but don't make it habitual.
4. As soon as the dog understands the lesson, ease up on the reward (food or praise), offering it less and less.

Normal everyday acceptable manners do not always earn praise. Your relationship with the dog and the bonding that develops your trust in one another are enough. Remember, every pat on the head, friendly glance, smile, spoken word is actually "praise" to the dog. It's easy to overdo it. Your boss may remind you a couple of times to shut down your computer, but he or she doesn't praise you every day for the next ten years for performing this routine function!

Bozo is completely over his man-in-the-hat phobia.

WHY OBEDIENCE CLASS?

I often hear dog owners complain that they did six or eight weeks of Obedience training and "it didn't work." As any trainer will tell you, six or eight weeks is just the beginning. One session of nursery school doesn't give your youngster much of an education either. That first course of instruction is to help you get started in teaching your dog. It's the parenting principle again.

You, the dog's owner, must learn the ropes before you can teach your dog. Obedience training of some sort is a *must*. You must have control of your dog to protect guests from muddy paws and kids from being knocked down, and above all for your dog's own safety.

Dog parents give numerous reasons not to attend classes.

I can do it myself at home. I just want a pet.
Half the point of attending class is to get you and your dog into a social situation, where an instructor can correct you *and guide* you *before your mishandling of a small problem gets out of hand. Pets with problems end up in pounds.*

Classes are too expensive.
A good eight week session won't cost anywhere near as much as replacing a chewed-up carpet or the vet's bill for saving a dog hit by a car.

My dog is already too bad. I'd be embarrassed.
You'll fit right in! That's how 90 percent of the first-time students feel.

My dog is six years old—too old.
A dog is never too old to learn. Keep it fun. Old dogs love the extra attention.

Rusty's just a mutt. I got him at the pound.
Rusty is a dog you *chose; he didn't choose you. Now is your chance to show him you want him to be on your team.*

To sum up, as one part of responsible dog ownership, you owe your dog an education.

Pets with problems too often end up in pounds. No excuses! Get Rufus into Obedience classes.

EVERYDAY OBEDIENCE

Your dog must trust you and want to please you by complying. There's no way to compromise with a dog. No promise of "if you do this, I'll do that" will work. Therefore, you are saved the youngsters' ubiquitous "Why?" Tell a dog to sit and it sits because you said so, no questions asked. Count your blessings! The trick is to *use* those user-friendly Obedience lessons on a daily basis.

How? Easily. Rufus is in the other room. Call him in an excited voice, and when he comes, reward him with a smile and command Rufus to sit. (Another smile; maybe a "Good Sit.") Now put him on lead to give you control and to remind Rufus of who's running this show. You're headed for the bedroom. Tell Rufus to Heel, then put him on a "Wait" while you go through the door. (The "Wait" may not have been included in the first six weeks, but be sure to add it soon because it is very useful.) Rufus can maintain a long Down while you make the bed.

"Okay" or "Let's go" when you're ready to do something else.

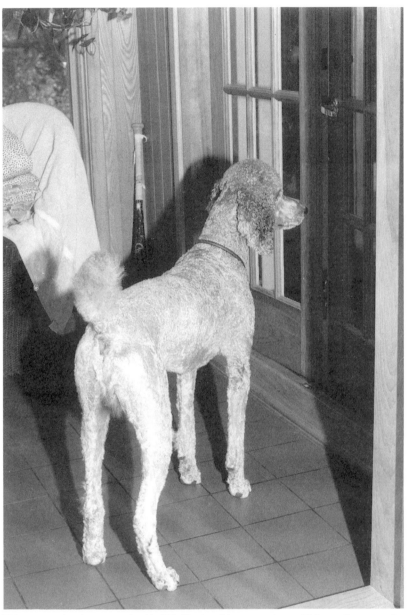

This trustworthy dog was asked to "Wait" when his owner stepped into another room for a moment and is waiting even though the door is ajar.

You're fixing a snack or a meal. Send Rufus to his "place" or "crate" (using the one word to indicate wherever you've decided he should be at mealtime). You're on the phone. Rufus can Sit-Stay or Down-Stay. (Or a trick! During one very long phone call I actually taught a dog to roll over on hand signals.) You finish your inside chores—"*Let's go! How about a walk for a good dog!*" YES! You did it! You're using dog talk.

As you can see, it is possible to use those Obedience lessons throughout the day, every day. If Rufus doesn't do as you asked, assume he didn't understand your request. Try again. Keep "No" to a minimum. After your next session of Obedience classes, Rufus will be off-lead and helping you with the housework! And all the time you'll be developing a bond of friendship and trust.

LANGUAGE SKILLS

As Rufus matures, add some challenges like a few hand signals for "Sit" or "Down"—very useful when you're on the phone! Have you any idea how many pet owners leave their dogs every day with the same two little words we dole out to our kids? "Be good," we say. When our dogs master our language, no doubt they'll come up with a smart response. But are our kids (who supposedly do speak the language) any better behaved because we've told them to be good? Do you believe in the tooth fairy?

We have no true IQ tests for dogs. Intelligence varies from breed to breed, individual dog to individual dog. We like to think that dogs who learn quickly are smart. Maybe they are, but probably not with any superior intelligence. They have figured out that pandering to us will bring the rewards they covet—a smile, an ear rub, a game, a dog biscuit. So failure to learn may have nothing to do with the dog's innate intelligence, but may be merely our failure to teach correctly.

If we're truthful (about our dogs?!) we'd have to admit that intelligence is just not that much of a deal. Good manners at home and away, loyalty, putting up with us when we're in a yucky mood, not shedding much, no doggy odor—those are things that really count!

A Sit-Stay makes a quiet (smiling!) companion during a phone call.

Single Words

Let's get back to language skills. The basis of teaching a dog is one-word association. Dogs build up quite an impressive vocabulary. For example: *No* (don't overdo that one), *Come*, *Sit*, *Stay*, *Down*, *Off*, *Heel*, *Wait*, *Walk*, *Outside*, *Car*, *Gooddog* (say as one word!), *Watchit* (also one word), AACHT, their name, names of family members and friends, food words (*treat*, *cookie*, *biscuit*, *dinner*, *drink*, etc.), specifically named toys, response to verbal alarm signals such as "Whoizzit?" or "Whawazzit?" Plus all those silly things we all love to teach our pets—and then to brag about them!

COPING WITH NOISES

All parents at one time or another must cope with bad dreams, "things" in the dark, "something" under the bed and so on as a child grows and the imagination develops. Cuddling, reassuring small talk and perhaps a night-light are some of the comforts we offer. We naturally extend such comforts to the fearful child.

Your dog's fears are often related to noise such as thunder, fireworks, car backfires, a gunshot, even a slammed door. Or they may be social fears—a lack of early exposure to strangers, different places, other dogs. These are really not difficult to deal with because the cure can be set up fairly easily.

The response to sudden noises is an instinctive animal fear, no matter whether you want to tie it to an inability to comprehend the abstract, or link it to a primordial instinct for self-preservation. *Animal fear does not respond to cuddling, small talk or similar human comfort devices.* These methods only reinforce the fear itself. In other words, if you use them with a scared puppy, you are in effect telling the puppy that it is okay *to be afraid*, that you approve of the fear.

This is one very important difference in parenting a child and a dog. There is simply no way to *explain* to an animal the source or the significance of a frightening sound or sight.

Puppies and other young animals will huddle together when afraid, but if you observe closely, they totally ignore each other even as they physically crowd to occupy a single space.

You may experience this behavior when the dog (regardless of size!) suddenly lands in your lap and sticks its head under your arm at the first clap of distant thunder. Proximity is all that's wanted. Not stroking, not talking, not petting or any other form of comfort as we know it. Here's a case in point and its solution.

Maxie, a large, strong male Rottweiler with a wonderful temperament became quivering jelly during a thunderstorm. His owner held the growing puppy's shaking form through one storm after another, offering verbal comfort. Then came the Fourth of July and Maxie destroyed almost everything in the room where he had been confined while the family went to see the fireworks. (This scenario is repeated in thousands of homes all over the U.S. every July 4th, by the way, as is the instance of terrified dogs running off and never being recovered by their owners.)

Maxie was cured of his hysterical reaction by the help of tape-recorded thunder, which was kept barely audible for several lessons while the smiling owner enticed Maxie to play with a huge plush duck, all the time using a happy, upbeat voice. The level of sound was *very* gradually increased over a period of several weeks.

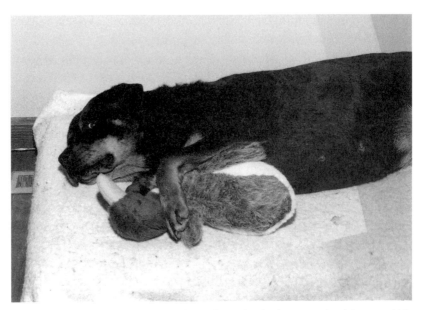

Maxie makes it through the Fourth of July fireworks thanks to good training—and his "storm toy."

Each time Maxie became the slightest bit upset, the sound was lowered, but the playtime with the toy remained. Success was assured when Maxie ran to get his "storm toy" as they called it. When he could tolerate a full-blown thunder storm, other noises were added that had visual connections—a dropped saucepan, a popped paper bag containing his ball, slammed doors. And finally, fireworks. This time the owner stayed home, only to watch dear Maxie sleep through the whole July 4th extravaganza with one paw on his "storm toy."

This method for solving behavior problems, sometimes called "saturation," will also work on other minor fears such as the man in the hat, the woman in sunglasses or whatever hang-up your dog has. Enlist as many friends as you can who fit the description (or can be costumed to do so). You sit with the dog on a park bench, on your front steps or wherever you and the dog are comfortable. Then these people your dog considers "monsters" begin to appear one right after another. You correct Rufus with a firm "Sit" or "No bark" only as necessary. *Never* say anything resembling "It's okay" because it most definitely is NOT okay for Rufus to be afraid, or to bark or growl at these people. He must be minding you alone.

Meantime, the parade continues in a nonstop round-robin. Hours later, when Rufus accepts them walking by, have each person stop, say hello to you and move on. The next step is to have each one speak to Rufus and finally each one will give him a tiny treat. Warning: This can take hours. Literally. Even days. You cannot rush the process. Choose your friends accordingly, and celebrate your success however you like!

One dog owner who followed this scenario said, ''Friend,'' each time a person came by. By the end of the retraining, her dog could look at anyone the owner called a ''friend'' and wag its tail! Cute trick. It cured the phobia, took some of the boredom out of the training process and added a very useful word to the dog's vocabulary.

Consistent discipline is important, and if everyone in the family adheres to the same rules, same vocabulary, your dog can be perfect, too. Child-care specialists agree that children, especially younger ones, learn best through repetition and consistency. Dogs, too.

A young puppy doing a Time-Out in her crate.

3

Time-Out

PARENTING

Primary parenting techniques for disciplining dogs and kids include:

1. Establishing routines
2. Laying down rules
3. Defining limits

Establishing the routine comes first because it sets the stage for everything else. With a reliable daily routine in place, Rufus begins to trust. Without a routine, and without trust, all discipline is an uphill battle. The closer you can stick to a set routine in the beginning, the deeper the trust and the better the dog will be able to cope with variations that are bound to arise in the future. Changes are part of life and dogs are extremely flexible, but *first comes routine*.

Laying down rules doesn't mean Obedience drills, just your own individual house rules. Young pups should not be allowed on furniture because they can and do fall off and break bones, but if you want your mature dog on the couch, so be it. If you think it's cuddly to have Rufus on the bed (and your sleeping partner, present or future, agrees), so be it. If you want to keep the dog out of certain rooms, make it a firm rule. Where Rufus goes to wait out your mealtime is a rule. Kids in the family need to be taught how to make the dog comply.

Good discipline and good parenting rely heavily on prevention. Keep that in mind when laying down the rules. If there is any way to prevent a *mis*behavior, the job of parenting evolves into the pleasant task of reinforcing acceptable behavior. My aunt had two dogs, one called "No-George" and the younger one named "Joy." When asked about the names, she answered, "It was just such a *joy* not to have to say 'no' all the time!" She had learned to appreciate prevention.

Perhaps you're familiar with the Persian Carpet Caper. Complaints about the destruction of possessions by dogs invariably place the emphasis on the monetary value of the thing destroyed, not on the cause of the misbehavior. The classic question is, "Why did the puppy chew my Persian carpet and not the old mat by the kitchen sink?" The answer is as obvious as it is simple: "Because it was there." The "it," however, refers to the puppy, not to the carpet. If the puppy or adult dog is not given the freedom to misbehave (in this case, access to the carpet) such catastrophes would not occur.

Sadly, most new dog owners think the pup only needs to be housetrained to qualify for what owners call freedom. And it *is* sad, because the owner thinks he or she is being kind to the dog (there's a bit of brag value, too). But that so-called freedom only means the pup is "free" to get into trouble and then to be punished for it. Saddest of all is that the puppy is punished for behaving like a perfectly normal puppy. The chances are a chewing incident would have gone virtually unnoticed had the old kitchen mat been the target.

In somewhat the same context, Mark Twain wrote, *"If you pick up a starving dog and make him prosperous, he will not bite you. This is the principal difference between a dog and a man."* Perhaps we should count our blessings that dogs do *not* put a monetary value on material objects (ours or theirs).

Prevent such calamaties as the Persian Carpet Caper by giving any dog new to you and/or your home, freedom in the house only under your constantly watchful eye. This should be done regardless of where the dog came from, its size, age or breed. (Those are just excuses.) Don't be in a rush to allow the dog to get into trouble all over your house! It may take a year or two to reach that goal. There are lots of individual dogs who can never achieve this kind of freedom for a variety of reasons, but they are delightful pets all the same. Their owners just know that confinement to kitchen or crate when no one is home means a happy reunion upon their return.

Perhaps now you can begin to accept the fact that much unwanted behavior in dogs (as in kids) is normal and nothing to be alarmed about. It's how you handle it that's important.

Two disciplinary measures for defining limits that work equally well for pups and toddlers vary only slightly in their implementation— *ignoring* and *isolation*, better known as *Time-Out*.

WHAT IS "TIME-OUT"?

The idea of giving a child a Time-Out is not really new, although the term may be. You may recognize it as the old-fashioned "Sit in the corner" or "Go to your room." It is pure Victoriana, dusted off, polished up, given a catchy name and hailed as modern. Time-Out has the inference of a tag line such as "and cool off" or "and think about it" or "and get your act together," which makes Time-Out a discipline rather than just a punishment.

We're all familiar with the Time-Out as it's used in many sports. Ice hockey has a penalty box where players spend minutes (we assume) thinking about their infraction of the rules. Other sports use a Time-Out to regroup their players or rethink strategy. Judges order a recess or Time-Out in a heated courtroom debates.

Time-Out for Dogs

This is a method by which you will teach your dog the boundaries of acceptable social behavior. When Rufus does not comply with your idea of what is "acceptable," he is removed from society for a brief period of time. A Time-Out must be given *promptly* (immediately!) and *often* (every time) so the timing is the same as for a punishment, but what's missing is the anger and frustration. When *you* are assured time to regain your composure, it's easier to control displeasure. With a Time-Out, everyone (child or dog, parent or owner) is given a few minutes to calm down. Then it's over.

Here are just a few of the advantages in using the Time-Out discipline.

THE DOG: is denied your company (essential to a dog) by a Time-Out. Because it is a no-nonsense, nonviolent form of discipline, the dog learns he/she can trust you to be in charge.

THE DOG: is given a chance to come into line. Caught in the act, the dog is given one "No!" If it doesn't stop instantly, the next step is Time-Out.

THE DOG: knows whatever he/she was doing at that precise moment was not acceptable behavior.

THE DOG: does not endure meaningless abuse (verbal, physical or emotional).

Like all disciplines, to be effective the Time-Out must be used consistently, in the same way, every time it is called for.

Where?

The ideal place for a puppy or young dog to spend a Time-Out is the dog's empty crate because it's escape-proof and boring. *One warning*: Because this is also the dog's den, bed and very own place, it is even more important when using the crate for a Time-Out that you show *no anger* en route. My dogs, for example, do not find it at all confusing that I use two different words to direct them to their den. Of course, the tone of voice is totally different, too. "Crate!" is used for any one of many reasons (sometimes accompanied by a treat), and they trot off, tails up. But when I say "Time-Out," tails go down, ears down, heads lowered and the submissive body language says it all. When mama ain't happy, ain't *nobody* happy!

Other Time-Out spots to consider are an exercise pen (toys removed), bathroom (rug, mat or towels removed), mud room. Any small room used for a Time-Out should have a pet (or baby) gate in the doorway.

In establishing a Time-Out place that is not escape-proof (only for an adult dog), begin with a very short time and remain in the vicinity so you can reinforce the "Stay" (but only as necessary— don't nag). A large, unruly black Labrador spends its "thoughtful moments," as the owner refers to it, smack-dab in the middle of the kitchen floor. What's more, the dog goes there instantly on the command "TIME-OUT!" The owner admits it took lots of pretending to be busy at the kitchen sink before the dog decided she meant it.

A very lively Welsh Terrier does this time sitting on a kitchen chair pulled well away from the table. The place you choose should be easily accessible for you and B-O-R-I-N-G for Rufus! Once you've decided on a suitable place, stick to it. Indecision on your part undermines your authority.

On the other hand, once you have taught the dog the Time-Out, you can use it wherever you happen to be. The only difference will be that you will take the dog to the spot where you want it to be for a couple of Time-Out minutes. Use it in a friend's house, in the park— anywhere that the dog's behavior goes beyond cute or funny.

Punishment of any sort is only as good as the lesson it has taught and must end the unwanted behavior. The dog must accept your disapproval and understand what must be done to earn your praise. Corporal punishment, in particular, is often too severe and administered in anger. Verbal or physical correction (the type used with a training collar) is too little (meted out by an easily intimidated, loving owner) or too late. (Unless caught in the act, it is too late.) In addition, many dogs respond aggressively to severe punishment or harsh training methods.

GROWLING

Signs of aggressive behavior often begin when the dog tests the owner. A well-mannered Standard Poodle started growling and snarling whenever the owner tried to retrieve a stolen object. The dog was now at the point of hiding under the bed with the forbidden loot clenched in a set of bared teeth. When Yannick was purchased as a six-month-old puppy, the owner admitted to having slapped the dog on the side of the head ("not very hard," he said) on many occasions for stealing socks.

"Fight fire with fire," decided this intelligent dog! Next time Yannick stole something and growled, his owner backed off, unsure how he felt about being bitten. Chalk up a major victory for the dog. Soon the dog was victorious every time, taking all the ill-gotten gains (T-shirts, socks, ties) back to the cave—well, you know, under the bed.

Growling is another one of those "things dogs do," like barking and digging, but it's important to recognize it for what else it is. *Growling is a warning signal* because the dog feels threatened, in Yannick's case, because the stolen treasure would be reclaimed. Punishment is not the answer when the dog warning you is in a stressful situation. In fact, punishment may be the worst thing you can do, because while it may momentarily stop the growling, it leaves the dog with unresolved tensions liable to erupt at any time into a potentially dangerous situation. Instead, eliminate the cause.

Is the dog growling at a stranger? Train slowly and gently until strangers are not just acceptable to the dog, but enjoyed.

Does the dog object to being touched? (Or the prospect of being touched?) Again, train slowly and patiently until the dog shows no stress at being touched and goes beyond simply tolerating it.

This whole procedure, used to modify many undesirable behaviors, is given a label by animal behaviorists that I find offensive. It's called "desensitizing," which I admit conjures up Nazi war crimes, but now if you hear a trainer or behaviorist use it, you'll know what it means. (See pages 43–45 for the "saturation" method of retraining.)

And what about our friend, Yannick? Apart from growling over loot, he was an easy dog to work with, so it didn't take long to overcome the problem. The first order of business was to make Yannick's owner conscious of where he dropped his socks and T-shirts! Then the dog was taught to "give it" using things that were not stolen such as large sticks, a wooden dumbbell and toys. Yannick, who had been on his way to the adoption block, took to the Time-Out method instantly. Oddly enough, the place chosen was in the corner of a room looking at two blank walls. Shades of the owner's childhood, perhaps! Anyway, the owner, whose pride had been crushed at being defeated by a dog, now pleasantly basks in their joint success.

Molly doesn't get away with stealing the baby's toys, but every now and then she tries. "Give it" gets the bunny back.

ANOTHER TIME, ANOTHER PLACE

What began as praise for being a good watchdog almost landed another dog in the shelter. By the time Scruffy was two years old, when anyone came to the door, his barking was out of control. The cure was to put the dog in the den across from the front door.

This was a Time-Out, but took into consideration the fact that the dog would be able to protect his tiny female owner if an intruder was at the door. In the beginning, Scruffy was crated in the den doorway. After many months, Scruffy caught onto this variation of the Time-Out, and when the doorbell rang, he raced into the den doorway and sat quietly.

Several years later, they moved to a ranch-style home with the den at the far end of a very long hall. Now every time the doorbell rings, Scruffy races the entire length of the hall to sit expectantly in the den doorway while his owner answers the door at the opposite end of the house. What began as a cure for unacceptable barking has become the dog's "pet trick."

Toby does his Time-Out in the middle of the kitchen, while the kids cool it in another room.

HERE'S HOW

In order to orchestrate the Time-Out effectively, the first thing you'll need to do is to control your emotions, including anger, frustration, fury and heartbreak (remember the Persian Carpet Caper). Once you have gone over the scenario in your head a few times and know precisely what you are going to do and how you're going to do it, try it out. Thankfully, dogs are not critical, so if you blow it the first couple of times, just keep your cool and try again the next time it's needed. The dog has to learn its part, and dogs learn by repetition. Practice!

Timing the Time-Out

You come upon Rufus, your four-month-old puppy, who has just overturned a wastepaper basket. (Remember not to make the big boo-boo of calling a puppy to come to you in order to be punished.) Go to the pup, say "TIME-OUT" in a firm matter-of-fact voice, and without any further comment lead him to his place, which, for a young pup, is probably the crate. Close the crate door and walk away. For a misbehavior of this type, it's better to go straight to Time-Out, rather than starting with the "No," because you need time to clean up the mess and your Time-Out voice can be used to indicate your disapproval.

If, let's say, you come upon Rufus *about* to put a paw or nose into the trash can, shout "NO!" in a growly voice. Wait a second or two, no more than that. If the pup stops, say "Good dog," and use a toy as a distraction. If Rufus stops, but you can't get in the "good dog" reward before he immediately returns to the trash, that calls for a Time-Out. He has done something wrong and has disobeyed you. *Two wrongs equal one Time-Out!*

Check-Out Time

After two to three minutes (about as long as it takes you to clean up the trash and take a deep breath), release the culprit, but only if the dog is quiet. If you use the release from a Time-Out while a dog is whining, barking or fussing, you defeat your purpose. The dog will have learned that whining, barking or trying to dig out of confinement must be what *you want*, because you come and let him off the hook! So when Rufus fusses, say "QUIET!" in your firm no-nonsense voice, wait a few seconds for it to sink in and then let him out when he has agreed to your terms—sounds of silence.

You can see how important timing is. It is far more important in dealing with a dog than with a toddler because Rufus only connects present action (his) with present reaction (yours). A toddler has a better memory for past transgressions! Your own voice combined with accurate timing are what teach a dog right from wrong, good from bad.

Consistency

We spoke of consistency and this is where it really comes into play. No matter how many times a day the pup breaks the rules, the complete Time-Out procedure must be followed from start to finish. It may take twenty-five trips to the Time-Out on Monday, and on Tuesday all misbehavior may stop in two.

Stick to it and don't forget that discipline is also teaching. At other times during the day (when the Time-Out is a thing of the past) ask the dog to do something you can admire, or just notice some good behavior you can praise.

Vary the length of stay in a Time-Out depending on the extent of the bad behavior (maybe combined with how long it takes you to recover!) and with the age of the dog. A puppy can stay in a crate or in a small space for three to five minutes, but you can't expect it to sit in the middle of a room for more than twenty seconds. As the puppy learns the Time-Out routine and matures (eighteen months to two years), you can extend the Time-Out to five to ten minutes. The actual length of time in isolation is somewhat variable, which makes it an exceptionally viable tool.

The side benefits of giving yourself these few minutes of space in which to deal with the situation will help you to put the whole thing in perspective. If you have small children, they probably understand how this works because the chances are you've disciplined them in this way. They will know, too, that you must totally ignore a dog that's on a Time-Out.

Some young children can assume the authority needed to send the dog on a Time-Out when necessary, but little kids (under the age of three) become dictators if given this kind of power. Also chatterboxes! Evaluate your own offspring honestly, and if you have any doubts, only put them in charge when you can supervise. Older kids should be taught to use the Time-Out correctly so Rufus has this consistency of discipline from the entire family.

Where Else?

Apart from the middle of the kitchen floor, a chair in the middle of a room, a blank corner of a room or the dog's crate, there are other good locations for a Time-Out. Using a gate in the doorway of a bathroom, laundry room or mudroom generally prevents whining or barking, especially with a puppy because it can see out. Also, it helps if you really need to peek in and see what's causing those strange noises, or to stop the fussing. The gate lets you do so without opening a door, which—to the dog—is the "okay" or release signal.

Just remember to think "boredom." This is not playtime or naptime! Neither is it an exercise in cruelty. You are disciplining by depriving the dog of your company and offering nothing but boring isolation to fill the void.

Don't Be Cruel

Some behaviorists recommend closing the dog in a dark closet for a Time-Out. I do not. True, it is isolated and, true, it is boring, but many puppies become very frightened and anxious in a dark closet, especially at the normal fear stages in their lives (such as five months). The point of the exercise is not to cause mental anguish but just a no-fun, boring situation as the direct result of a misdemeanor. Besides, how many closets in your house are completely empty or even partially puppy-proof? You could be trading off one misbehavior for another if half the contents of the closet are destroyed during what should be the cooling-off process of a Time-Out.

You will also need to decide which unacceptable behaviors actually qualify for a Time-Out. For example, a pup that whines, cries,

Sitting in the corner is humiliating—and boring for Fancy. A perfect Time-Out.

58

howls or barks when you leave the house is exhibiting unacceptable behavior, but it will not be corrected by a Time-Out. Such a pup is having an anxiety attack from being left alone. Separation anxiety requires patient teaching, or behavior modification, to overcome.

If you left the dog alone and not confined while you went shopping and came home to find your bedroom destroyed, *you* will need a Time-Out. But this is an instance where the dog will *not* learn anything at all because the discipline comes too long after the misbehavior. However, the dog will be spared your understandable anger and frustration. Next time, remember confinement is kinder than freedom to get into trouble.

JUST SAYING "NO" ISN'T ENOUGH

Many dog owners run into problems because they don't understand why the dog won't respond to their shouts of "NO!" It always boils down to a case of "No" just not being enough!

When "No" is the only discipline given, it doesn't get the job done. It's only one-half of the exercise. Think of "No" as an initial warning to a dog that has already learned what a "Yes" is. One "No" coming from a scowling face is followed by teaching what's wanted. When the dog breaks a rule it has already been taught, the one "No" is followed by a Time-Out. "No" can be used as a "Don't even think it," but *only* if the dog has been taught right from wrong. "No" can easily become just another nagging word. Charlie Brown of *Peanuts* once commented, "I need more hellos and fewer goodbyes." I think Snoopy might have said, "I need more good dogs and fewer nos."

TIME-OUT FOR KIDS

A mother told me once that she felt if kids were raised right, they would respect animals. Therefore, when her children pulled the dog's ears, she pulled theirs; if they yanked on the dog's hair, she yanked theirs. Experts in child behavior do not agree with this negative, tit-for-tat method of discipline because it so easily leads to bullying.

Time-Out for a large dog is an enforced Sit-Stay with a short leash attached to a hook in the door-frame.

Use a positive approach, and if little Liza Mae is feeling particularly ornery, give her a Time-Out. Afterward, explain to her how we do treat friends like Rufus, gently and lovingly. Some things take longer to teach toddlers. Kindness to others is just one of those things.

Your puppy or newly acquired older dog (like any little kid) will test you and every other available person until firmly told to knock it off in a way the dog understands. Both dog and child need the same secure safety net of boundaries set up by someone who is fair, nice to be around, in authority and consistent. These things provide an environment of caring and establish trust. Two-way trust is a vital ingredient in your life with a dog. It's what makes the relationship special.

MUSICAL CHAIRS

There are lots of individual ways to make use of the Time-Out. Simon, a Sheltie, was obedient and loving, that is, until his owner sat down. Then the dog raced around the room barking and nipping at the owner. The "alpha roll" (turning the dog on its back and having it stay there until relaxed) had been tried for several months and was not working. Then Simon was put in a Time-Out a minute or two *before* the owner went to sit in his favorite chair. I won't fool you. This was not an instant success!

The dog met the new challenge head-on, but his owner was equally determined to make it work. Simon had to be put back in his Time-Out corner over and over and over again, and when the fight finally went out of the dog, Simon tried persuasion. When the little yips and cute cocked head didn't work either, Simon at last waited out the time in silence.

Following the Time-Out, it was especially important to ignore this dog because any attention at all provoked another demonstration. It was not a happy household during the training period, but Simon's owner can now walk into any room, tell Simon to sit (on the floor!) and then settle into any chair he likes in peace.

OLD DOGS—NEW TRICKS

And don't think that Time-Out is only for puppies and young dogs. Doreen's dogs were twelve and five years old when the older dog started snapping at the younger one.

Lots of dogs get crotchety as they become senior citizens. They hang out the "do not disturb" sign and mean it. A Time-Out gave the old guy some peace and quiet and it separated the two without punishing either one. Additional walks gave the younger dog a physical outlet and some much-needed individual attention.

DON'T THREATEN—DO IT!

Use the Time-Out immediately for a major misbehavior. When the infraction is minor, give one warning "No!" and if that doesn't stop the action instantly, go straight to a Time-Out. Any pooch worth dog biscuits will quickly latch onto how many nos add up to a Time-Out! Be sure to let Rufus know it is no more than one, and sometimes none at all (which will actually help teach respect for the "No" when the dog hears it).

END OF TIME-OUT

Now comes the hard part. Play it cool when the Time-Out is over. Release the dog with whatever one word you select. "Okay" is good because you can use it to end other things, too, like a Down-Stay or a Wait. It is oh, *so* easy to succumb to those enticing paws, pleading eyes, playful yips and funny antics. It helps if you keep reminding yourself that the pup is *not* sorry. Trixie is trying everything in that bag of tricks to get your attention and by doing so will have won round one of the next match! Her own mother would ignore her. You must, too. Continue to ignore until she is no longer trying to win you over, then welcome her back in your good graces with a smile, a walk, a pat on the head, whatever you like.

Ignoring is so difficult for most pet owners that the next entire chapter is devoted to the subject.

4

The "Ignoring" Principle

HOW GOOD ARE YOU at ignoring your dog? Be honest. Most people find it almost impossible. Dogs are such good attention-getters that they can pull a "gotcha" before we know what hit us.

Besides, part of the reason we keep dogs as pets is for these endearing, if somewhat infantile behaviors. The pawing that says, "Let's go for a walk." The soft pleading look that clearly means, "Oh, come on, let's share your snack." The little yips, the whines, the nose-nudging, the pulling on the pants leg or sweater, the *crash* against the back door (meaning "Outside NOW!"), the toys that get dropped into your lap, the wiggling beside you on the couch (nosing your evening paper aside)—all these things, and all those other cute things that *your* dog does, demonstrate the numerous ways in which the dog manipulates you.

Separate the few that are a true means of communication, such as the bark to go out, the alarm bark to tell you Dad's home (or the

The pawing that clearly says, "Put down the paper and let's go for a walk!" The reply is ignoring. A persistent pooch may need a Time-Out followed by ignoring.

house is on fire), rattling the dish to let you know it is dinnertime regardless of what the clock says. Separate those, and ALL the rest are attention-getting manipulators. That's not to say they are wrong or that you should eliminate them, because I know, you know and all dogs know that it would be next to impossible to do. But you can make use of these same antics to manipulate the dog when needed.

Dogs even play these attention tricks on each other. Two of my own dogs each have a "place" in the dining room. Badger invariably grabs the corner bed, which for reasons known only to the dogs is the preferred location. Bittersweet tolerates this briefly and then pulls her manipulative trick. She turns on her alarm bark and dashes toward the front door. Badger also wants to confront demons at the door—but instantly Bittersweet turns on one paw and hops into the corner bed with a smug look on her face. True to all objects of manipulative behavior, Badger never ceases to fall for this one. Now, if I could just teach *him* how to ignore!

Exactly the same sort of thing goes on in every household between dog and owner. It can be funny, but not always, and not at your expense! Use it only as needed, but do learn how to ignore.

Ignoring is one discipline that can be used *in*consistently, when you are not trying to eliminate the act forever from the dog's repertoire. Ignoring works on all friendly, cute little behaviors that are not bad or even naughty (some are even funny) but that can on occasion be annoying and are definitely antics that allow the dog to be in charge. A tiny Chihuahua begging for a crust of toast may be cute; the chin of a Bullmastiff on your plate is not! The first can be solved by ignoring, the second requires firmer discipline.

We teach a dog physically, for example, by placing it in a desired position, and mentally by the use of verbal commands. We also teach a dog by prevention. Perhaps the method most overlooked by pet owners is the vast amount we teach dogs by our own *body language. Ignoring is the intentional use of body language.*

When you discipline by ignoring, you are telling the dog that you will laugh, love and be happy with these attention attractors some other time, on your terms. You're letting Star know you're onto her.

HOW TO IGNORE

Every now and again, just say "No!" to the one attention-getter you find even a little bit annoying. There's usually at least one that is more of a pain in the neck than cute, at least sometimes. If the annoyance doesn't stop immediately, go to the Time-Out, but when you release the dog, ignore her. That's a lot harder than just saying "No." Do you really know how to ignore an adorable dog who, among other fantastically true things, is telling you how absolutely *mah*-velous you are? Well, here's how.

1. Do not look at the dog. Not even a sneaky peek. Do not speak to the dog. Not even one derisive word. (Especially not a comforting word.)
2. Do not touch the dog. Not even one tiny pat. If you are sitting down, push the dog away from you with your book or newspaper. (Careful now. *No kicking* or physical abuse.)
3. Gently move the dog aside without a word, without eye contact. This is not the time for an "Off" command. This is ignoring!
4. If you are standing up and the dog approaches you, fold your arms in front of you and turn your back. Walk away if necessary.

At this point you are probably saying to yourself (or to Star); "I don't want to ignore all those sweet little things!" If so, you've missed the point. This is where the "we're all human" part comes in. Don't even try to eliminate all those antics that make your dog different from every other dog. You certainly aren't going to turn away or say no every time the dog says, "Hi, how are you?" But Star does need to know you can't be had so easily. Ignoring allows you to enforce discipline now without jeopardizing your options to saying yes or no in the future. Ignoring tells the dog that right now you have better things to do or other priorities. Ignoring is clear canine language that says what it means: "Back off!"

Let's say you put up with the dog jumping all over you whenever the two of you meet. You are armed with excuses. "I'm only wearing

A persistent pooch gets the ultimate in ignoring.

jeans," "I like a dog who makes a fuss over me," etc. Then comes the day when you're en route to a breakfast meeting with the boss, dinner with a date or cousin Sid's wedding. Do you think for one minute Star is going to stand back and admire your outfit? Or believe you if you say no only on this one occasion? Of course not! Unless a dog has been disciplined or taught that her behavior is mostly acceptable but *sometimes* isn't, she's going to jump all over you and pay no attention to your pleas, which may escalate into a screaming tirade of verbal abuse. (See? We've all been there!)

The corrective "No" is a constant and may be followed by any one of a number of reinforcements (Time-Out, "pin," end of play, distraction, etc.). Whereas ignoring, used inconsistently, strengthens trust, establishes your rights. It's a flash card that says: NOT NOW. DO NOT DISTURB.

The ignoring you use after a Time-Out, let's say for growling or chewing the kitchen table, enforces the isolation treatment and tells Star that she must earn her way back into your good graces. Ignoring, as we're discussing here—to put minor attention-getters on hold—is flexible.

When Star is firmly told, "No," she stops what she is doing. Star is then ignored for awhile, and learns that you are not always a total pushover. If you let yourself be easy game for the dog's ploys, she will be endlessly seeking your attention and trying to see just how far she can go before reaching the limit of your endurance. Every now and then, let her know she has reached it!

DON'T IGNORE DOMINANCE

Not all demands for attention are signs of a sweet, loving, kow-towing temperament. Some are quite the opposite. They may be an indication of a dog with a deep-rooted desire to maintain dominance.

For example, when pushing aside the small dog trying to get your attention during "ignoring", you should *not shove* or use excessive force. A dominant dog might react to such physical abuse by biting. In case you think otherwise, dominance as a character trait comes in dogs of all sizes!

On the other hand, I feel dominant dogs have suffered from a bad press. Matched up with people who can appreciate their somewhat independent attitude, they are actually more interesting dogs to live with because of their stronger personality and their confidence in knowing exactly who they are. This is not always a good choice for children, however.

Ignoring can also be used as a follow-up to a Time-Out or a severe punishment that needs some reinforcement of your disapproval. The dog must be totally ignored after the Time-Out and you must stick to it to be effective. If you only ignore for a minute or two and then give in, the dog will not only have won that round, but also will remember precisely how to do it. Star will be ready to defy you the next time you try to ignore her no matter what the reason.

If you give in, you are actually rewarding the dog's MIS-behavior. Let your displeasure sink in until Star stops trying to break your silent treatment.

This is not excessive or cruel. It is pretty much the way dogs themselves handle a member of the group that gets out of line. When the wrongdoer gets the message, she gets back into the pack's good graces by demonstrating restraint or moderation plus showing acceptance of the leader's mandate. Ignoring is a putdown that hits home.

An ignored dog typically puts her head very quietly around the door to the room where you are. She's testing the waters. It's the old throw-the-hat-in-the-door trick. Ignore it. Another ploy is to do something really cute, like dropping a favorite toy at your feet. It's the candy-and-flowers approach. Ignore it. Ditto alarm barks to tell you there's a monster at the door. Walking into the room directly behind (or even beneath) the kids is another ploy often used by big dogs and meant to break the ice.

You alone must be the one to end the period of ignoring when you are good and ready and Star is suitably subdued. Do it casually. Suddenly switching from ignoring to rewarding (be it verbal, physical or nutritional) is not the way to go. Be imaginative, even devious. Go into the bathroom for a few minutes, and come out returned to your normal self. Or step outside on the pretext of taking out the garbage, getting something from the car—anything, so long as it is without the

An ignored Frosty is testing the waters.

dog and without speaking, and casually return to normal (noneffusive normal) upon your return.

Don't be surprised if Star follows you around like Mary's little lamb for some time after this treatment. If so, she's got your message. Good! She's paying homage. Don't reward this action. As I've said, "ignoring" is a behavior modification used by older dogs or those of higher rank to keep subordinate upstarts in their place. It is language all dogs fully understand no matter what the age, rank or serial number.

OTHER ATTENTION-GETTERS

Somtimes a dog will have exhausted all the cute things and will turn to such things as house soiling, which affords the dog prolonged attention! Negative, verbal abuse, but attention nonetheless. Unless caught in the act, go right to a Time-Out followed by ignoring, but make some changes. For example, confine such a dog when not supervised, give additional exercise and tone down *all* other forms of attention.

Ignoring, isolating, using the Time-Out will not turn your dog into a wimp. On the other hand, these things will help your dog to understand where you draw the line between acceptable and unacceptable behavior. Since this is a mild form of discipline, it will also save your vocal chords and your frustration.

AN EXTENDED TIME-OUT

Use ignoring after a Time-Out, especially if you yourself need a longer Time-Out than the dog! Child psychologists believe that parents are guilty of giving a disruptive child too much attention before, during and after the disturbance.

This also applies to disciplining our dogs. Dogs can be taught to understand an average of twenty one-word instructions, but when these are incorporated into superfluous verbiage, the all-important single cue word for the desired behavior is lost. Prattle is pure verbal attention. The dog either bathes in it, or reaches for the "off" switch.

Star doesn't need to hear *why* she did something wrong, or *why* it upsets you so much, or *what* it will cost to replace, or *what* you will do next time! Following the Time-Out, for further emphasis, ignoring makes your point.

BARKING BACK

Playful puppy barks or yips are mere chitchat. We're talking "barking back." It's the same as the back talk or sassing that young children use to test their power. That's just what the pup is doing— trying to find out what the owner's reaction will be. Toddler and puppy part company pretty quickly on this, however, because the curt "No" from a two-year-old fifty times a day may be bearable, whereas a person's tolerance for barking may be limited by the volume or pitch of the bark, or even by how much the neighbors can take.

The toddler says "No" and waits to see how her parents react. Parents are counseled to remain calm. Unfortunately, when the young

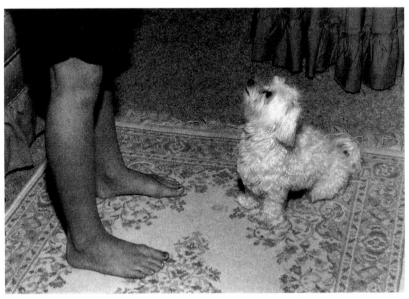

Barking back is what got Frosty into trouble in the first place!

puppy barks back, most people are enchanted by that expertise. Laughing, smiling or a mere glance of approval encourages the puppy to keep the bark back in the bag of tricks. That's asking for trouble in the months ahead.

Barking back is defiant. You say "Come" and Star stands eight feet away, looks you right in the eye and barks. It's the "make me" attitude. Invariably it takes place at home, not in Obedience class, which is exactly the same scene played out by the youngster who feels secure in venting defiant behavior within the family, but not so confident on the outside. Barking back starts in the puppy, and that's just where it should end.

LISTEN UP!

Barking is one part of every dog's language. If you had wanted quacks, you'd have bought a duck. In time you'll be fluent, but in the meantime, here are some basic barks with their translations.

Barking back: Sharp, defiant barks usually delivered standing, looking you right in the eye, but not threatening, often with head cocked to one side as if asking a question, but actually it's a "No" in response to a given command. Enforce the command!

Playful barking: Short, staccato barks or yips usually combined with the down-in-front, up-in-the-rear body language that is an invitation to play. No correction needed.

Barking to intimidate: Medium-strong and consistent against cornered prey that, for the domesticated pet, may be a ball or other toy stuck under the couch. Eliminate the cause.

Barking to give chase: If a cat or squirrel is not around, a vacuum cleaner or leaf rake will do nicely! This requires "no bark" training.

Barking for attention: Often a small, whiney sound used when asking to go out, where's dinner, to sit on a lap, etc., and often accompanied by pawing. Temper it by ignoring as necessary and by noting what's essential and what isn't.

Alarm barking: This is the respected call of the watchdog. Often it does not occur until maturity. In some breeds it's hysterical and high-pitched, in others it is stronger, sharper and louder than any other bark.

Pawing is a puppy form of begging. If you allow it to continue, the pup will still be pawing at twelve years of age!

There's no mistaking it! Respect it and always investigate the cause, but teach Star to stop when you say so and to trust you to take over.

Howling: Some breeds also include howling in their repertoire. We don't fully know why they use this form of communication except perhaps because it may carry a longer distance than the bark. Northern breeds (the sled dogs) and scent hounds howl more than others. Dogs of any breed that are tied up for hours or left outside at night are predisposed to howling. Dogs rarely howl if their people are around.

In the case mentioned of a pup barking back in defiance of the "Come" command, the way to handle it is first to remember NEVER again to call the dog unless you are in a position to enforce the request, leash attached! Negate your own command by turning and walking away, ignoring the dog and therefore denying *any* response. Give it a moment to sink in, and then use a distraction. In the house, open the fridge or a cupboard, pick up the dog's toy; outdoors, begin to run in another direction. Then, as the dog (being a naturally nosey curious puppy) comes toward you, say "COME-good-dog" (almost as one word). Keep this pup on leash until you graduate from Middle School.

DEFIANT BARKING

Attempts to punish for defiant barking won't work. It's like the situation with the pre-schooler who tries to get her own way. Unless you are firm from the beginning, the pleading and the begging (the barking) turns into that time honored game of "yes-you-will" "no-I-won't," which Ginny has already won the second she roped you into it.

Barking back is a puppy tactic, but there's a Peter Pan in every crowd and some dogs remain puppies forever, so best get this potential problem ironed out right away. Getting angry only gives the puppy negative attention, but if the only way the pup can get attention is to bark back and get yelled at, then the dog, like the toddler, will settle for angry yelling, shouting or similar abuse.

Of course, this is *why* ignoring works so well with a dog. Any attention is better than none, and ignoring is nothing. Thus the dog comes into line quickly. When you wisely use the discipline of ignoring *some* of the time, you'll then have the control you need for specific times. Ignoring alone will not eliminate an undesirable behavior, but it will reinforce a "No" or a Time-Out. To the dog it says "Knock it off" loud and clear for small nuisance behaviors. It's a top-quality, easy-to-use, no-cost training tool, and you always have one with you.

5

The "Spoiled Child" Dog

EVERYONE KNOWS at least one spoiled child who wheedles, whines and fusses to get his or her own way, who always wants to be the center of attention and who is indulged, never disciplined. No doubt you've witnessed the scene at the check-out line where little Bobby whines, "I want candy." "No, you can't have candy," says Mom. "I want gum." "No, you can't have gum." Voice goes up two octaves: "I WANT BUBBLE GUM!" At this point, his mother tries to make a deal: "Okay, but only the pink kind." Voice now up to a screech: "I WANT PURPLE!" Bobby was offered what he *said* he wanted, but all the child really wanted was to find the limit. Temporarily, the attention he was getting by changing goals was enough for him.

The child-substitute dog often operates the same way, and for the same reasons. He demands attention and gets it. But when met with nothing but consent, the demands skyrocket because what the indulged pet or child needs and seeks are solid boundaries. You are not being cruel or depriving the dog or child of love by setting limits. Quite the opposite. You are providing the essential safety fence that says "I care."

Pet owners are often amazed when made to realize just how demanding their dogs are. Many of the devices used to gain attention reflect infantile behavior. Such things as pawing, whining, licking (especially around the face) are all young puppy behaviors that continue so long as they bring about the desired result.

In the very young puppy, the behavior is directed at the mother to elicit feeding and protection, and may be transferred to the human caregiver for a short time. The pup exhibits this form of submissiveness to all adult dogs. But in the case of an adult pet, because food and care are freely given, and the dog has no need to be submissive, the purpose of these actions is solely to gain more attention. Just another example of why it is so easy to become overly emotional with pets. Their childlike dependence on us is part of their charm. People need to be needed and a dog fills the bill nicely.

THE ONLY CHILD (READ: DOG!)

Here is a somewhat modern parenting problem: the single parent (read: dog owner) whose social life has for the past two or three years evolved around an only child, which in fact is an only dog. Suddenly this nice, kind, all-attentive owner begins to date.

Having been retained as reigning monarch in residence, but without good social skills, the dog takes this sudden change in lifestyle as the ultimate in culture shock. The poor dog is stressed out.

Should Rufus attack the intruder, thereby earning praise, approval, maybe an extra hors d'oeuvre for protecting his alter ego? Should he play Joe Cool and just happen, always, to come between these two people on the couch? Perhaps try a distraction—like knocking over the lighted candles, or asking to go out? Or maybe this calls for the maximum canine revenge: lifting a leg on the interloper! The female version of this is to leave a definitive message on the owner's bed.

Should he play Joe Cool and just happen to come between them?

It's an enormous problem for the indulged dog, and one that is invariably handled poorly by the owner. The last thing he or she needs to cope with is a neurotic dog!

SOLUTIONS

There is one obvious solution. Prevention by means of good parenting disciplines saves time and frustration down the road. So it's Monday morning and the game is over for this person. What can all the rest of us learn from these mistakes? Prevention!

Prevention (1): Young puppies (or newly acquired older dogs) need to be socialized as soon as possible after adoption with many different people, in many situations, at home and away.

Prevention (2): Never dote so much on a dog that it cannot tolerate sharing your attention, your physical proximity and your affection, or that it cannot trust you to make changes.

Okay. You didn't do (1) or (2), so now you need to make some radical changes. The spoiled dog, like the spoiled child, did not get that way all by himself. You, the owner, created this—and didn't the little darling learn quickly! Now you'll need to be your cheerful, friendly self as you gradually but firmly gain back some of the ground you've lost. Begin by remembering, no matter what your feelings, no matter how beguiling the appeals, you are dealing with a dog. A spoiled dog maybe, but your basic dog.

Don't get me wrong, however. Spoiling is not necessarily all bad. Lots of us need to feel we can be indulgent, so if we can't indulge ourselves or our kids, then why not the dog. What one person thinks is overindulgence is just an extra dog biscuit to someone else. It's only when behavioral problems arise that *spoiled* becomes *rotten*.

JUST WATCH ME!

There's a phrase taught by Obedience instructors, ''Watch me.'' It is used to keep the dog's attention on the trainer while awaiting the next command. Once the dog has learned to respond to this, it's useful for getting the dog's attention. It's exactly how the overly indulged dog operates. By using physical and vocal attention-getters, as ''Watch me,'' and only varying them to fit a given situation, the dog has trained the *owner* to ''watch me.''

One example of this is the bark a dog gives to let you know it needs to go out. A smart dog will soon have you on your feet and heading for the cookie jar instead of the back door! A pleading whine (just like the kid at the candy counter) will probably persuade you to share a piece of toast. Nibbling or tugging on a sleeve or pants leg is another cute way for the dog to say ''watch me.'' The child pulls similar tricks. Pawing, nudging your arm or jumping into your lap are also effective from the dog's point of view. Sometimes just staring is enough of a ''watch me'' on the part of the dog to get your undivided attention.

''Alarm barking'' is another strategem many dogs latch onto. (See also Chapter 4.) Performed in an empty kitchen, for instance, it will bring you on the run certain that at least the dishwasher has exploded. What the dog does next depends on its ability to think

Newspaper-nudging, another attention getter.

fast. Sometimes it's followed by "let's go for a walk" antics, or "as long as you're up, how about a treat?" Or, for the dog with an evil sense of humor, it's just a plain "gotcha!" It's the toddler's scream for mama! Or perhaps the boy who cried "wolf". Effective though, isn't it?

WHO CONTROLS WHOM?

Once you start counting up all the ways your dog controls you, you'll know which demands you want to keep (barking to go out and legal alarm barking are obviously in this category) and which you can begin to tone down or to eliminate. Every pet owner puts up with numerous things that another pet owner would find intolerable. The choice is yours. Spoiling a dog to react in unacceptable ways (with fear, growling, biting or barking) is unkind to your dog. These are infantile reactions. You need to let your puppy grow up (regardless of its true age).

Make a list of *all*—no cheating, now—ALL of the things your dog does to make you respond, keeping in mind that eye contact is a response, as is a kind word or one brief pat.

Then tick off the attention-getters that are essential, which will include the various things you have purposely taught the dog. Now look at that long list of nonessential, manipulative leftovers! Cute, maybe, but some may be making your life, to say nothing of your dog's life, miserable. An overindulged, spoiled dog is *not* a truly *happy* dog. Because this is an unstable dog it cannot be trusted, nor can it trust others.

ONE-WORD COMMUNICATION

Begin by *paying less attention* to the dog. (*Ignoring* as if you hadn't guessed!) Shorten some of your conversations to one-word communications the dog can understand. If Rufus doesn't know these words now, he soon will. In fact, he will learn very quickly that *he* now has to watch *you*, or do without attention altogether. It's really an easy choice for a dog. Dogs are smart. They know where their cookies come from!

"Sit" means on the floor, not your lap. "Wait" means the dog stays in place for a moment, for example to let you go through a door first, and waits for what comes next. "Off" means "get down off," but we *use only one word*, so "get down" is implied and silent. "Off" the couch, the chair, the bed, that nice other person who just walked into your life. You may feel your Canine Queen has had her day, but male or female, it will be a far happier *dog* with life simplified by knowing *you* are in control.

In addition to the emphasis on a one-word vocabulary, put other attentions on hold. Reduce the sweet talk, the fondling, the extra treats. It means you will occasionally ignore the dog, which is healthy. It tells the dog there are other things in your life. It means you are allowing your dog to be a dog. A child does not want (or need) a parent as a peer pal, and a dog doesn't want or need an owner as an equal. Lead, follow or get out of the way, but don't try for equality with Rufus. (Forget what you see on TV with those highly trained dogs in the hands of skilled professionals).

There is one problem that arises in connection with an overly pampered dog that has to do with the size of the dog, not the amount of indulgence. When a small dog is carrying on, for example when meeting someone on the street or at the door, there is a great temptation to pick the dog up and to offer quieting comfort to calm the outburst.

That is where everything goes wrong. (This is, as I said, a small-dog situation. Since a large dog cannot be picked up, the resulting problems don't occur either.)

For example, the tiny dog barks, growls and snaps when the door is opened for guests. The owner picks up the dog and (invariably!) coos, "Oh, it's all right, Precious, it's just the Smiths."

Now there are THREE problems. By picking up Precious, the dog's physical stature has been raised four or five feet above that of even the largest canine! This gives your small dog a totally false sense of importance. That is the first thing wrong with this scenario.

The second is the tone of voice used. You *cannot* verbally *explain anything* to a dog. While it is possible to comfort a child by using a calm, reassuring tone of voice even if you are murmuring sweet nothings to a nonverbal baby, it is not so with a dog. All the dog grasps is your *approval* of the act. It's precisely as if you were saying, "Oh, you are a good dog to growl and snarl and carry on when our guests arrive!" It has exactly the same effect as a smiling "Good dog" when the dog does exactly as it was told.

The third point to consider is that any stressed-out dog held in your arms could very easily bite you in the face. Yes, even your little darling! Spoiled or not, it is still a dog, and under stress dogs bite whatever is available.

Call a Time-Out to put everything back in proper perspective. Follow this by lessons in how to say hello nicely. (To review the Time-Out method and how it works, see Chapter 3.)

"ME, ME, ME!"

The puppy (also the "status" of the spoiled dog no matter what its actual age) and the toddler share a pair of beliefs: Everything is "Me!" (or "Mine!") and "Now!" These are considered to be the inalienable rights of the extremely young. Each is self-centered and operates in the present tense. There is no sense of sharing, and no tomorrow.

The primary purpose of the "me/mine" attitude is self-preservation, whereas sharing is a social behavior reached through discipline and example. It is a social skill taught in day-care centers, nursery schools and elementary schools everywhere. For kids, it takes maturity to accept. For wild animals it's a question of sharing the kill or being killed. Not so with the pet. The innate concept of community property to little kids or pet puppies is that time-honored law: "What's mine is mine, and what's yours is mine."

Sad to say, the dog relates to past and future only through learned experiences. For example, the dog connects the jingle of your car keys in the morning with your departure, but *not* with the fact that you'll be back after work. So the idea of "future" is a learned behavior, i.e., the connection of something in the present (keys) with the result (your leaving), a learned routine. The concept is not truly "future" because once you have gone, rather than being secure in the knowledge that you'll return at six o'clock, the dog may in fact undergo stress or separation anxiety; or the dog may just relax in the present and spend a peaceful day following the sun around the house.

Note that it is still in the framework of "me" and "now." This is not to refute the well-known fact that many dogs have built-in timers. They sense when the kids' school bus is due or when Bob gets home from work, when it is almost dinnertime! But not the time concept of "the kids will be home in an hour." Dogs do not sit around all day anticipating the future event. (At least we are pretty sure they don't!)

As for sharing, the dog *learns* not to snap or growl over a toy when playing with a person. But because the dog *is* an animal, and because it never completely outgrows the "me/mine" attitude, a growl warning just *might* be tried if the circumstances make "me/mine" stronger than the learned "Give it." Two dogs, for example, do not automatically share toys, or treats, or space on the couch. For this reason, two otherwise compatible dogs might never tolerate being fed side by side.

The dog learns a routine, and learns to share to a degree, but "me/mine" and "now" are always just beneath the surface. Dogs look for immediate gratification, which is one very good reason to teach a dog to "Wait." The dog learns to associate that command with a short-term future. "Wait" is a "now" word so the dog can cope. Your intimated ". . . and I'll tell you what to do next" is perceived in a general way but only after many satisfactory conclusions to "Wait" have taken place. So we're right back to square one, because the way the dog figures it is, "If I wait here *now*, something nice will happen to *me*."

All these me/mine/now behaviors are based in self-preservation, which is why even the domesticated dog doesn't outgrow them, and retains a portion of these attitudes even after extensive training. The child learns substitutes that work better, and are more self-satisfying or rewarding in a civilized adult society.

THE WORKING OWNER'S GUILT

Avoid every conceivable form of guilt you may feel because you must leave the dog alone all day. This is a fact of your life (or your lives together) and not something you need be upset about. Any feelings

"Wait"—and maybe I'll open the door.

of guilt will have one of two adverse results: Either the dog will become increasingly spoiled by your unwarranted attention when you're around or will come under stress because of your emotional departures.

Quality time, not overcompensating for the lack of it, will let you and your dog share an enjoyable relationship. Discipline the dog as needed, punish or correct as needed, use Time-Out and ignoring as needed and then sit back and put your trust in your canine sidekick. Stroking your dog at the end of a day's work will do wonders for your blood pressure and for the dog's well-being. Unless you're a glutton for punishment, throw away guilt and all negative counterparts.

DOG WALKER

There are so many latchkey pets today that a new group of job opportunities has opened up to fill a real need, and they include everything from dog walkers to day-care centers (sort of nine-to-five boarding kennels). If someone walks your dog in the middle of your workday, be sure they are familiar with the key words that have specific meaning to the dog. Also inform them of any special disciplines you want maintained. On the other hand, there's nothing wrong with letting Rufus think this surrogate walking partner is a pushover for an extra few minutes of play or a second treat. (See? I'm not 100 percent against spoiling. But note, in this instance the treats come from someone other than the owner.) Just as you would for a regular babysitter, leave your work phone number and that of your veterinarian.

HERE COMES THE COMPETITION!

Adding a second dog to the household before correcting the problems of the first spoiled dog can spell disaster. It can even spell danger. A dog living by attention-on-demand does not give up the numero uno position all that easily. LeRoy (Rufus would never!) must now maintain authority over his owner *and* the new upstart. That is regardless of size, breed or age. (As you can see, this is a big, full-time job even for the dog who has everything.) Unfortunately, it can be so stressful to LeRoy that the stress turns into aggressive, jealous behavior culminating in a classic dog fight.

Careful thought should be given as to why a second dog is being considered. Sometimes a second dog is added for the wrong reason.

Faulty Reasoning

Rusty is lonely—he needs a playmate. (But Rusty may think everything is just fine and dandy as it is—he has it all. At five years of age, why should he learn to share?)

Or, the owner thinks it would be fun to have two Rustys. (No two dogs are alike, any more than people are. Parents often don't like their kids' choice of pals—Rusty may hate yours.)

You had two dogs before you got Rusty so surely you can manage two dogs now. (Those two dogs were littermate pups. You never owned an older dog. You were twenty years younger, and your mother trained and cared for them. *Be Real!*)

A second dog would give Rusty more exercise. (Destroying the house? Or more likely you will have two couch potatoes.)

Subtract First, Add Later

For the sake of peace, love and happiness, start to wean that dear, sweet Rusty of his exclusive rights to your life before thinking of adding a second dog. When the dog accepts that change, you can begin to contemplate what life would be like with two dogs.

Breed enters into this picture, too. Some breeds of dogs are more laid-back than others about accepting a second pet, be it dog, cat, bird or gerbil. But, bear in mind that the *spoiled* dog defies breed type. It is a spoiled dog first, and laid-back Labrador or active Chihuahua second. There are many dogs (spoiled or not) that are extremely territorial and will only tolerate the intrusion of another pet if the owner is fully in charge of that particular transition.

Mixed breeds can be fine pets, but they offer a nondoggy person virtually nothing that's predictable, and such a person is in dire need of knowing as much as possible what to expect in regard to size,

Frosty and his kitten companion.

probable temperament, inherited and environmentally acquired characteristics, trainability, etc. Not everything is a given when you opt for a specific breed, but the element of chance is *greatly* reduced.

If One is Good, Two is Better

Multiple dog ownership is not for everyone. That's not a put-down, but a fact of life. We can't all be Olympic athletes, or movie stars, or ride a horse. Some people cannot cope with the responsibilities or the problems of owning more than one dog at a time. One of the main reasons multiple ownership does not work out is the erroneous application of a human rationale: "If I can love three dogs, they will love each other and we'll be one big happy family." Maybe—and that's a *big* maybe.

"Love" is a very small commodity in the animal kingdom. A working relationship built on respect and trust is closer to the dog's version. Tolerance is usually as good as it gets, and edgy tolerance is a time bomb with a short fuse, leaving the loving owner nonplussed at

89

the failure of the venture. As I've said before, think of multiple dog relationships as in-laws, not long-lost lovers!

BUT . . .

Maybe you are still saying, as you possibly were at the beginning of this chapter, "But I *want* my dog to be a child substitute." Or, "My dog *is* my child." Okay. That is your choice. However, you might consider whether or not that would be your dog's choice.

Dogs that are allowed to be dogs are enjoyed and appreciated especially for their dogginess, and are also the ones that do *not* end up in shelters as castaways because of behavioral problems.

So if your dog is your "child" and that's the way you want it, at least give him or her the opportunity to behave like a dog sometimes and enjoy some dog activities. You may be in for a surprise . . . you may actually like your dog better when you get to know this other side.

Heather was a city dog. She lived in a skyscraper and was carefully walked on city streets so as not to get dirty. She was a spotlessly white West Highland White Terrier.

One day she was chauffeur-driven out into the country to attend an American Working Terrier Trial, or "dig," where small terrier breeds of the right proportions go into a long dark tunnel nine inches in diameter to locate a (safely caged) rat at the end.

Heather's owner had not counted on several things: It was pouring rain. The tunnel floor was mud. The place where all dogs and owners awaited their turn was a large, cold, drafty, hay-filled barn. Heather and her "mother" chose to wait in the warm car. Their turn was quickly moved up before they could escape back to the city.

The pale-blue suede collar and leash were removed and the Den Master took Heather out, in the rain, to the opening of the simulated woodchuck tunnel. As the dog's feet hit the mud, she was into the tunnel in a flash, found the caged rat and in good terrier fashion barked her head off. Following that success, Heather and a couple of the other terriers created mayhem when they located a rat behind bales of hay in the barn.

Heather went back to the city on a borrowed bath towel spread on the seat of the limousine, mud from nose to tail and a sparkle in her eye that certainly was not there when she arrived.

What can we do? Oh, let's write about a dog—a really smart black dog.

I don't really know what her owner thought of all this, but those of us terrier aficionados at the event were delighted to have seen Heather discover her true identity.

That is simply one incident in one group of breeds, but it points up the fact that dogs were bred for specific jobs. When people turn them into pets, dogs too often join the unemployed. Keep this in mind when your dog looks bored, gets fat and his or her only job is to ''be good.''

There are many activities available now to give dogs at least a taste of the real reason for their being. There are tests and trials for tracking and retrieving (land or water), every imaginable kind of hunting, herding, lure coursing for sight hounds and the terrier trials mentioned. And don't overlook just basic Obedience, which can be put to use every single day of a dog's life as a means of friendly communication, persuasion, or self-preservation.

A little boy once asked me at a dog show what my dog could do. The dog was entered in show competition and I told him we hoped she could win a rosette. ''Yes, but what can she *do*?'' he asked again. I

A puppy gains confidence with Mom's guidance while the kids watch. Soon it will be their turn.

92

put the dog through a few Obedience routines and added a trick or two. The child was sort of satisfied, but I sure wasn't! He didn't know it, but that child helped launch the dog's breed-specific career that summer afternoon.

No longer is there any excuse for having a dog that doesn't "do" anything. There are plenty of things for them to do everywhere.

Most of these job projects, by the way, require little or no work on your part beyond basic Obedience. The dogs do the work; that's the whole point. Like the kids, the dog will require transportation to and from the event and the sign-up fees to be paid by mom or dad. The rest is fun, entertaining, a social experience and quite an eye-opener for anyone who thinks all dogs do is eat, bark, ask to go in or out and take up space on the couch.

Still not convinced? Still want your lapdog (size has nothing to do with the phraseology) doing nothing more than gazing adoringly into your eyes? So be it. Enjoy.

A minimal reminder for a very large dog.

6

Puppy Basics
(Older Dogs, Too)

THIS CHAPTER will cover preventative measures for
the new puppy owner to follow so the normal antics of the puppy won't
become problems. *Don't skip the chapter because your dog is no longer
a puppy.* One thing dogs have going for them (and for their owners)
is their ability to be *re*trained when previous training went wrong,
including all the bad habits they picked up by themselves. Behavior
problems in the older dog can often be corrected just by going back to
"puppy basics." I won't kid you: With a corrupt older dog, it will
take longer, with much patience. There are a few exceptions, but it's
not an impossible task. There's little chance of success, however, if
you hitch your wagon to all the exceptions, or cling to excuses. Go
about it with a positive attitude and your dog will share your outlook
and success.

HOUSE AND CRATE TRAINING

These two subjects—introducing the dog to your house and to a
crate—begin with you, not the dog.

Your house, be it a twelve-room country mansion or a bed-sit in the city, is something upon which you and you alone must place the value. A dog's idea of real estate is quite different! *Possession, not appraisal*, is the way a dog looks at it: What's mine is mine and what's yours is mine if I can get a hold of it.

In order to teach respect for your property, you need to be around, so the first order of business is to decide how and where you will confine the dog when you are NOT there to supervise normal canine inquisitiveness. For most people, the kitchen is a good place because the furniture is minimal, the floor washable, rugs removable, newspapers on the floor tolerable and access to a fenced yard immediate.

A pet gate will keep most dogs confined to the kitchen once they are taught that it is a barrier to be respected. Don't put up a pet gate, install Star in the kitchen and go off to work innocently expecting to find everything in the same place and condition when you return! Some dogs learn to respect anything (even the edge of a carpet) as a boundary beyond which they must not step. Others think of it as a challenge: to be climbed over, chewed up or dug out of.

TEACH, *don't punish*! Dogs that are crate-trained are generally also receptive to pet gates. The trick with the gate is to teach the dog never, ever to jump against it or to try climbing under or over it.

The easiest way to show a puppy what you have in mind is to lean the gate against the doorway so it will fall over with a crash if the pup should "forget." The noise will also bring you running so you can reinforce your point. "Oh, NO!" (as you replace the gate) is enough if the puppy backed off. However, if Houdini slipped through after the gate was down, give a sharp, scowling "No" and put pup and gate back in place. Whenever you see the dog ABOUT to jump against the gate, you can shout a very stern "NO!" For a persistent pooch, balance one or two Stop-It* cans on top of the gate.

Peggy, a full-sized adult Rottweiler, now obeys the visual bound-

---

*This simple device goes by many names and is widely used by trainers. It's nothing more than an empty soda can containing a few pebbles or pennies, used as a disagreeable noise distraction to tell the dog "whatever you are doing this instant, STOP IT!" which is why I call it the Stop-It can. It can be used to stop barking or digging (thrown on the ground near *but not at* the dog), or stealing (balanced or tied by thread to food or trash can). Very useful. Keep several handy in different parts of the house.

96

ary of a ruler on the floor in a doorway. They started with a pet gate when Peggy was three and one-half months old, switched to a yardstick leaning at an angle across the doorway and ended up with an old ruler. The benefit of this admittedly extensive teaching is that the twelve-inch reminder can be placed in *any* doorway and Peggy complies with the "silent rule." It's the old maxim: Use only as much discipline as is necessary for the desired result. The result in this case with such a large dog and such a tiny barrier does provide a few amazed chuckles, too.

CRATES

Over the last ten years there has been a great improvement in the pet owner's conception of the dog crate. It really only took two things to change people's opinion. One was semantics. The now-universal use of the word *crate* instead of cage. (We do not "cage" members of our family!) The other has been the acceptance of why the crate works. Dogs are den animals and are therefore secure in a crate-as-den. So dog owners were now able to understand the numerous benefits of the crate. When you consider the fact that we accept all the baby safety paraphernalia—the playpen, crib, carriage, stroller, car bed—it's no wonder pet owners want all those things for Star. They get many of them rolled into one: a CRATE.

Crates come in two basic styles, molded plastic (sometimes called an airline crate) and open wire. Each has a plus and a minus, so the choice is yours to make. Wire crates let the pup see out on all sides and you can see in, but need to be covered at night and wherever there's a draft (hot, cool or cold). The molded plastic is solid with wire "windows" on the sides and front door. They are draftproof and don't need to be covered, but most come with temporary cardboard flooring that must be replaced by a permanent grid floor or piece of Masonite cut to fit.

Size is more important than style. The adult dog should be able to stand up, turn around and lie down. Think small! It's a den, and 95 percent of the time your puppy or grown dog is in the crate, it will be sound asleep, curled up in a ball. Bigger only means the pup will sleep in one corner and use another part of this apartment as a bathroom.

A molded plastic crate offers a secure den and protection from the direct draft of the fan.

This puppy is just learning how to go in and out of the crate by himself.

Introducing the Crate

Introduce the pup to the crate by tossing a treat or a toy into the crate for her to follow, accompanied by lots of happy talk. Friendly persuasion is fine, but NEVER *push* or shove the puppy into the crate. And never slam the door shut as the pup goes in. Leave the door open until the pup will go in and out on her own. Praise when Star goes in. No reward (no comment at all) necessary for Star coming out.

As the pup is about to enter, say with a big smile, "Crate" (or "Bed"). Finally, "Good *crate*" as you now *calmly* close the crate door. Stay in the room for a few minutes *ignoring* the pup. If you keep looking at the dog, I promise you, she or he *will* kick up a fuss. If there's any barking, whining or digging, say "NO" sternly just once and then *ignore* it. Let the pup out only when there's no fussing. Gradually increase the time the puppy stays in the crate, and begin going in and out of the room, staying away longer and longer until the pup can stay put quietly (probably asleep) for half an hour or more.

Use the same procedure for an older dog, although it may take as long as two weeks to accomplish the acceptance you'll get from a puppy in a couple of days. If your dog is casual about food, feed her in the crate. However, do NOT do this with a dog that's aggressive about dinner, as it may increase that unwanted behavior.

HOUSETRAINING

Begin housetraining using the crate, taking the pup outside, on-leash, to relieve herself last thing at night. Then it's into the crate with a small good dog good night biscuit. The crate may be in your bedroom if you wish (advisable in the case of a very young pup, so you can hear the first morning call). No conversation—it's bedtime.

First thing in the morning (which for the first week or two may be earlier than you had in mind), take the pup (quickly!) on-leash to a designated spot outside. On-leash so you are there to give praise *as* she eliminates. Supervised play with you or the kids, inside or out, comes next.

The schedule is up to you, but the young puppy will follow one that goes something like this, in round-robin fashion:

Eliminate—Play—Eliminate—Sleep

Eliminate—Eat—Eliminate—Sleep

Sleep is in the crate. The pup will let you know when she or he wakes up and you can make good use of that whining or barking to teach the word *outside*.

Eliminate is outside, unless you want to paper train or have a Toy breed and will be using newspapers or a kitty litter box.

The ingredients for a happy puppy:

- Playtime is an important opportunity to enjoy, to love and to begin teaching.
- Feed the puppy (two to four times a day, depending on size and age) in the crate if you have other pets or small children.
- Keep a bowl of fresh clean water available for the dog at all times. Lick bottles (often used for hamsters and gerbils) are okay *if* licking doesn't bother you, because it does tend to encourage the habit.

- Do *not* put water in the crate where it will spill and leave the puppy with a soaking wet bed. Small children *can* be taught not to touch—honest!

The pup will gradually slip into your schedule and decrease the number of meals per day as she matures (and the corresponding number of trips outside).

BACK TO REALITY

After a week's vacation, or a long weekend, when all this initial puppy training took place, you may have to return to work. Leave Star confined to one room, with the crate door *secured* in an *open* position (so she doesn't get trapped for the day) and with a few different safe toys. If the pup was ever trained to use papers, leave newspapers on the floor in one corner or by the door you use to take the dog out. Leave a radio on a light-music program at very low volume. Be sure all electric cords are out of reach, all kitchen cabinets closed, scatter rugs and trash removed. In other words, do everything you'd do if you were leaving a toddler in that room just for a moment. Then go off to work and hope it all looks somewhat the same when you return home.

The crate lets you give the pup its first lesson in trust (you sometimes lock the pup in, but you also let it out) and in accepting your authority. But the bottom line is that dogs like crates because they feel secure in a denlike atmosphere.

MORE ON CRATES

Once a pup has been taught to enjoy the crate, you will find more and more uses for it any time you want the dog safely, happily and quietly in one place for a few minutes up to a couple of hours: in the car, visiting family and friends overnight, during parties (especially children's birthday parties, which tend to be noisy and active) or when you've just washed the kitchen floor. This, of course, includes the Time-Out.

A safe place until the party's over.

Wire or plastic crates can be innovatively disguised in a variety of ways. For example, enclosed in wood frames to serve as end tables by a couch or chair, or fitted under a countertop in kitchen or laundry room. A young girl keeps her Shih Tzu's crate in her bedroom, complete with a lace canopy that once adorned a doll's bed.

When your dog is crate-trained, you'll be pleasantly surprised at the reception she gets from others. Your veterinarian and hospital staff won't have to cope with a stressed-out dog if Star has to stay a night or two. The staff at the boarding kennel will love you, and Star will get extra attention because she's no trouble. "Have crate, will travel" becomes your password when you want to go to Grandma's or Aunt Em's. All travel and visits to strange places are less stressful to a dog in the beloved crate.

As we discussed, the crate-trained dog has a Time-Out place if no other place can be found. *This is not just a puppy training tool.* A crate is a lifelong den; even if you end up with a fancy color-coordinated designer dog bed for every room in your house, hang onto that crate and use it at least occasionally—for any of the above reasons.

FREEDOM TO LIVE!

Dog owners have a fixation with "freedom." They want their dogs to have "freedom of the house" or think all dogs need "freedom to run." Well, in this day and age, what our pets need more is *"freedom from danger"* and *"freedom to live!"*

A dog that is allowed to run through the house unsupervised before being taught what she can and cannot do, and before being mentally ready, is only being given "freedom" to be punished. It's totally unfair to the dog and you will have lost ground in your teaching trust. Many happy, older, well-adjusted dogs (mine among them!) are routinely confined to one or two rooms when left alone in the house for any length of time.

"Freedom to run" has a wonderful, idyllic "Lassie Come Home" connotation, but in our society, it might better read: "freedom to run away" or "freedom to be run over." **More dogs die from**

being hit by cars than from any single cause other than euthanasia in shelters. Give Star the "freedom to live" by keeping her in the house when you can't supervise, and on-leash or securely fenced-in outdoors.

CITY KID

The "child substitute" puppy is often an apartment dweller. One owner had a problem housetraining a puppy because the dog was so frightened of the noises on the city streets.

She couldn't redirect the traffic, nor could she ask the puppy to hang on until they made it to the quiet park area two blocks away! But she did find an alleyway to use until the puppy overcame the fear. She took the pup there in a matter-of-fact manner, with *no* coddling or consoling. She said a cheerful "Good dog" as the pup eliminated, and then, with a squeaky toy and happy chatter, they walked quickly to the park where the pup relaxed and played. About a week was all it took for the puppy to begin to accept city chaos.

The owner's attitude was what made the solution work. No matter how many times I say it, it bears repeating: All your emotions—fears, anger, anxiety, sorrow—go right down that leash to the dog. This form of communication is more direct and accurate than fax!

Cleanup

This is a good time to mention cleanup. Lots of cities, towns and parks have ordinances about curbing your dog or being fined. Regardless of the law or where you live, picking up the poop is better than curbing.

There are several types of hand-held scoops on the market, or you can use plastic bags. Check them out at your pet store—but don't leave home without one! Put several in the car, too. For the backyard there are utensils made for the purpose (for grass or hard surface, for the feces of large dogs or small).

ELEVATORS OR STAIRS

Elevators can be a problem for a city dog. Star can be stepped on, and react aggressively either out of fear or to protect this small cubicle of moving "turf." Pick up a small dog so it isn't stepped on, but guard yourself and your fellow passengers from a possible fear bite. Keep the dog at waist level. "Sit" a larger dog in a corner and put yourself in front so the dog won't be stepped on or crowded.

Until Star is accustomed to the elevator, she may panic because the "flight space" is virtually nil. Don't coddle or sympathize, just make many (unnecessary!) trips up and down over a period of days until your dog can relax. On entering and leaving, watch out for a tail that could be caught in the door!

Lots of dogs have to be taught to go up and down stairs. Pity the dog that is wary of stairs whose home is a fourth-floor walk-up! When it's part of life, they all learn. Some need to be taught gently and patiently, one step at a time.

DANGERS

Anything you'd keep away from a toddler, keep out of a dog's reach. This includes all the disinfectants and cleansers in the kitchen, electrical wires, anything that should not be on the floor such as children's small toys, paper clips, rubber bands, bits of string and so forth. They can cost a small fortune to remove surgically. Love your veterinarian, but who needs this!

COLLAR AND LEASH

It's essential for the dog to tolerate a collar and leash for safety's sake. Show young children *indoors* how to hold the leash so it is comfortable and safe for them and for the dog.

A choke/slip collar is a training collar and can be extremely dangerous for the dog in the hands of a young child. REMOVE choke/slip collars after a training session and use a snap or buckle type for every day. Remember the puppy is growing and will probably need a larger size collar every few months until about one year of age for small to medium dogs, or two years for large dogs. Remember to move the dog's license, ID and rabies tags from the old collar to the new one.

CAR SAFETY

There are child safety laws as well as constant media warnings regarding the general safety of children in cars. There aren't any laws to protect dogs in cars, but perhaps there should be, for the dog's safety and also for the saftey of the driver and passengers. A bouncing, barking, claustrophobic canine is a hazard to everyone on the road.

Parents are all too familiar with the special car seats mandated for babies and young children. Building the child's safety seat into certain models has even become a major selling point for car manufacturers. Not many dog owners are as conscious of the variety of car safety items available for dogs, or if they are, they are not as conscientious about using them. These devices are meant to save lives—yours as well as your dog's. Use them.

Barriers

A car barrier installed in a station wagon will keep a large dog (or a hyperactive one of any size) in the back. In most sedans, it can be installed to prevent the dog from jumping into the front. Barriers are available in pet stores and through pet-supply catalogs. One word of caution: Be extremely careful about opening and closing the car's windows with automatic control. Many a paw, nose or kid's hand has been caught in windows closed automatically from the driver's seat.

Seat Belts

A canine seat belt is the answer for dogs who like to ride up front. There are styles to suit all sizes of dogs. For the most dangerous practice of all modes of travel, riding in the open beds of pickup trucks there are special safety devices that are easy to install and to use.

Everyone buckles up! Queenie wears a seat harness. There are various types for different dogs and cars.

Crates

The dog crate is the perfect car safety device. It can go on a car seat or in the back of the wagon or pickup, anchored so it doesn't slide or shift. It is "perfect" because if your car were involved in even a minor fender-bender, the dog can't escape if a door should fly open, or if someone comes to assist you in an accident. A frightened dog trying to defend the owner is not something to mess with. Many a rescuer has been badly bitten in an attempt to extract the dog's owner from a car crash. Many a dog is lost or killed on the road as a result.

Again: Think snug den, not condo. A crate that is too big is neither safe nor comfortable because the dog will be thrown about as the car goes around curves, brakes or accelerates. A crate that fits the dog correctly will also remain stationary due in part to the dog's weight being evenly distributed. If the crate is too large, the dog won't feel secure and in fact won't be secure.

A Beagle named Bunny panted, jumped up at windows, drooled, whined and flipped around inside the car on every trip. I suggested a crate and told the owner how to use it. Unfortunately, the owner thought she'd be kind to her active dog and get a larger size than the one I recommended.

She followed the advice for crate training in the house and all went well. But using the crate in the car was a disaster! The crate was first put in the back of the wagon, then on the backseat, but Bunny continued to pant, drool, whine and run around in circles in the over-sized crate.

Bunny wanted security not space. A few trial runs using a plastic crate in the right size (leaving the large wire crate in the house) and the Beagle soon became a happy traveler.

Don't Hang Your Head

It is just as dangerous for a dog to stick its head out the window of a moving car as it is for a toddler to do so. Dogs that are allowed to hang their heads out of a moving vehicle will sooner or later get road grit in their eyes and ears, requiring costly veterinary care. They can also get tossed out on a sharp curve, or hit their heads hard enough to do serious injury, if it's necessary to slam on the brakes. "My dog loves to do that" won't pay the vet bill. Precaution is cheaper. Be a responsible driver and a responsible dog owner.

In the Heat of the Day

Beware of cars in warm weather! It doesn't take a heat wave to kill a dog inside a car. On a mildly warm day, 75 to 80 degrees F., even with windows partially open, **the temperature inside a car can go up high enough to cause fatal heatstroke in a matter of minutes**. Regardless of age, breed, size or any other excuse that comes to mind, the fact is a car is a steel death trap for a dog (or baby) in warm weather.

A quick stop at the grocery store where, once inside, *you* can enjoy air conditioning, is all it takes for the dog to suffer permanent brain damage or death. Leave the dog at home, or if Star must be with you, secure her in the crate, leave the car in full shade and the windows wide open. And then, be quick!

Heat warnings also apply to cutting back on exercise (cut it down to nil when it's hazy, hot and humid). Sunbathing is for early spring and fall. Dogs don't get suntans, they get heatstroke!

Cold weather has another set of rules. Don't make your dog out to be macho. In bad weather house pets come indoors when they've eliminated or been exercised. Dogs that are kept outdoors most of the year should be brought in (at least to basement or garage) when temperatures dip, when snow or storms are predicted and for the WHOLE winter when they become senior citizens. Wash off ice and road salt from feet and underbelly and dry the dog thoroughly. And, just as you keep Star away from the air conditioner, in the winter keep her away from any source of heat other than sunshine.

SOCIALIZING

Dogs are social animals and enjoy being with people as well as with their own species. There are noticeably fewer behavior problems in dogs that have had ample opportunities to interact with others of

Kindergarten Puppy Training class. It's a family affair.

their kind. The isolated stay-at-home is the dog that's ripe for canine neuroses.

Some breeds are known for their steady temperaments, which only means that in general these pups will be easygoing, friendly, accepting of life as it comes. Unfortunately, some breeds are known to be skittish, shy, overly submissive or what might be thought of as the reverse—*hyperactive*, an overused word that usually means the owner bit off more canine activity than he can now chew! No matter what the individual genetic makeup, your dog still needs to be around a variety of people and other dogs in order to develop the social skills we humans require of our house pets.

Kids are great social companions for puppies, but if you don't have children, or can't borrow some gentle, obedient ones from the neighbors, get your puppy into mixed human company and by all means find your nearest Kindergarten Puppy Training classes (nursery school for puppies three to five months of age).

A school playground in rural or suburban areas can be a good source of kids, adults and other dogs. Don't let your puppy get mixed up in the team practice session of the moment, but do circulate among the spectators who are probably younger siblings, parents and other dogs. Let the pup's reactions be your guide as to how much of this is enough.

A normal "fear period" occurs at around five months, similar to the pre-schooler who hides behind Mommy's skirts rather than say hello to the teacher. So don't be a pushy parent, but you can encourage the pup to greet people and other dogs by giving Star plenty of loose lead. Pulling back on the lead is a mistake commonly made by people who think they are protecting their puppy. It can actually increase or even cause unwanted behavior (such as fear) in an otherwise outgoing pup. Older dogs will read the pup's body language and note that this is a harmless, nonthreatening puppy. They'll make their ritualistic canine greetings and move on.

I am not in favor of large supermarket shopping areas or shopping malls for socializing puppies. The atmosphere is excessively noisy, busy and just plain overwhelming to a pup. Being threatened, or terrified, does not impart social self-confidence to a child or a dog.

HOW MUCH IS TOO MUCH?

We have covered the pup's safety, general good manners and socialization. Exercise is essential, but the age of the pup and the breed or breed-type has to be taken into consideration.

Jogging with a twelve-week-old puppy is not smart (regardless of how great the brag value!). Bones, muscles and organs are growing at an alarming rate and all are easily damaged by overexertion. For a young puppy, play is usually sufficient exercise (particularly games of fetch, which most pups love), gradually adding walks, and very gradually increasing the length of the walks.

Any happy dog will run until it drops in order to please you. It's up to you to monitor the dog's health, strength and age, and to set limits accordingly. We can't all be competitive athletes, so be sure a veterinarian checks your dog thoroughly after you indicate your athletic intentions.

HEALTHY AND GORGEOUS, TOO!

Your veterinarian will tell you when immunizations are due. These physical checkups and vaccines are a lot cheaper than treating the illnesses, many of which can be fatal to pups. After the series of "puppy shots," it's an annual event. The so-called "permanent shots" are only permanent for one year. Rabies shots given after a dog is one year old may be good for three years.

Weekly grooming sessions will keep your dog (and therefore your house) clean, and make you aware of anything that may need the vet's care. It's easier to groom a pup, especially a fidgety one, that is off the floor on a picnic table or bench, or even on a stair. Get the puppy used to grooming so that when fully grown, and maybe huge, your dog will stand nicely for you anywhere. It's a time for smiles and friendly persuasion. Animals enjoy being groomed, but no mama wolf ever pulled out the electric clippers or nail trimmers! Easy does it.

Grooming includes brushing the entire dog—under the elbows, inside the hind legs, under the tail—checking for fleas and ticks as you go. It includes:

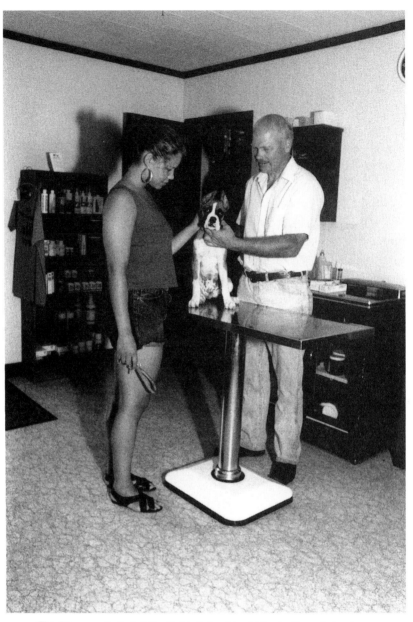

The Boxer pup's first visit with his "other" best friend—the veterinarian.

- wiping out the inside of the ears (gently, with a clean dampened tissue for each ear)
- cleaning teeth (special dog toothpaste and toothbrush, or baking soda on gauze pads)
- wiping the corners of the eyes (gently, with a clean dampened tissue for each eye)
- checking between the pads of all four feet for pebbles, burrs or other foreign objects
- cutting nails at least once a month

Breeds with long coats require regular shampooing (and *much* rinsing); breeds with fancy trims need professional grooming three to six times a year. Puppies of these breeds benefit from getting to know their groomer at a very early age, just to meet the person and get used to the sounds and smells of the shop, *long before any professional grooming is necessary.*

JUMPING UP

Most jumping up is a nuisance behavior, but with a very large dog, it verges on catastrophic. When any boisterous pup or adult dog jumps up on a small child or aged or infirm friends and relatives, you have a dangerous situation. Frankly, I love to have my dogs give me a rousing, jumping-all-over welcome. We are delighted to see each other. But even if you, too, enjoy the interaction, teach Star to respect "Off!"

As the dog jumps up, grasp one front paw in each hand and (still smiling and chatting) squeeze only enough to make the dog fidget and try to pull away. *Timing is important. As* you let go and *as* the dog drops back to four-on-the-floor, say (still smiling) "Off! Good dog." That's the first part of the trick. The other part is to do the first part *every* time the dog jumps up. Eventually Star will learn what "Off" means and the dog will choose to respect the word rather than have her paws held uncomfortably.

All right, you have a small dog and you love being greeted by jumping gyrations. Teach the "Off" routine, and separately (other

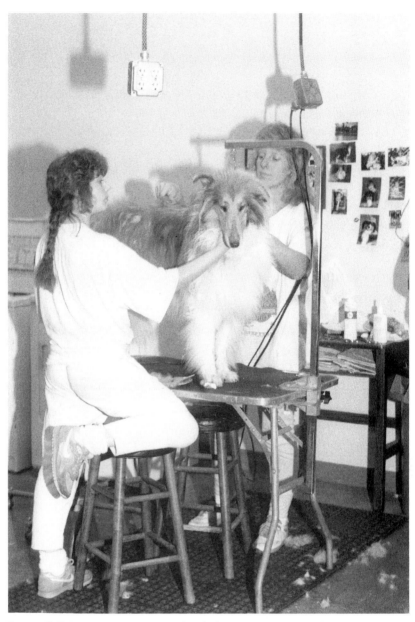

Even a Collie's puppy coat can get ahead of a pet owner, but professional groomers come to the rescue and get the mats out.

Johnny has taught his dog to "Give me five!" They're both enjoying the fun trick.

than when the dog is greeting you) teach another trick. "Give me five!" Keep your hands wide open when you make contact with the paws while you do a little dance and then it's "Off! Good dog." You are still in charge, but you can have the cake and eat it, too.

In either case, with friends, relatives or kids, attention is given when Star is complying with a nice Sit.

PART TWO

Dogs *and* Kids
The Family

7

Babies with Dogs

HEY RUFUS, GUESS WHAT?

Today's household is likely to have a dog in residence before the first baby arrives. The concerns about that resident dog's reaction to the new baby and the problems of adding a new baby to the household often have a common denominator: the dog has been a child substitute and, to a greater or lesser extent, spoiled. Just *how* spoiled will determine the degree of difficulty the parents encounter in introducing a baby person into the family. This may or may not cause a few problems for the dog, but is always (and rightly) a matter of some concern to first-time parents.

Be realistic. You have five or six months in which to restructure the dog's way of life. Don't waste a minute! The longer you wait, the more you'll be thinking of the baby, not the dog. Most of the preliminary retraining applies to Mom, but Dad needs to know what's going on in order to play by the same rules.

And baby makes three . . .

DOING THINGS DIFFERENTLY

Start by weaning Rufus of your attention. This doesn't mean you should suddenly pretend the dog doesn't exist. Far from it. Be aware of the number of times a day you play slave-parents to your dog's attention-getting devices, and begin to cut back your number of responses. Now is a good time to reread Chapter 5.

Figure out roughly what your new daily schedule will be when the baby arrives and begin to make changes in the dog's routine. This may include your being home all day instead of at work. It may soon mean an afternoon nap and now is the perfect time to reinstate the crate (or bed) as Rufus's place for a siesta instead of curled up next to you. Don't look at this as a form of punishment and Rufus won't either.

More important is the fact that this small form of separation from you (and putting the dog in a more appropriate place) has no connection with the baby as far as Rufus is concerned. Rufus can't misinterpret new procedures to mean ''Just because of that darn baby, I, Rufus the

120

great one, have to go to my bed in the afternoon.'' It's just you and your much-loved canine doing things *differently*.

Moderate walking is good healthy exercise before the baby arrives, and Rufus will enjoy going along. You might want to test your skills at negotiating an empty stroller or baby carriage and the dog (on-leash). If you can't manage it easily in your own backyard or driveway, do NOT try it by yourself with the *baby* and dog. This is new stuff for all of you, so you need to teach the dog to walk nicely *on-leash* next to you *now* before baby makes three.

If you happen to have a sled dog (one of the Huskies, or Northern breeds), watch out! It may awaken all natural ambitions to demonstrate that pulling you and a stroller is why this dog was put on earth! Very small dogs can run around and around under the carriage until they, you and the baby carriage are literally all tied up. Walking the baby may bring out the ''guard'' in your guard dog. This is a noble idea, but you don't need to be protected from every friend who wants to stop and admire your baby. Dad, Grandma, Aunt Em or whoever is around gets to help in retraining Rufus.

. . . or four!

PREPARATIONS

Let the dog share in getting the baby's room ready. It's a mistake to make the baby's area entirely off-limits to Rufus. Encourage him to investigate each new piece of furniture and equipment with you. Obviously, you won't allow the dog to get into the crib or on any other furniture. "OFF!" is your one-word command. By introducing Rufus to all this stuff now, by the time the baby arrives only *the baby* will be new.

Put a baby (or pet) gate in the doorway of the baby's room *now* to serve as a visual reminder that this room is visited by invitation only. Again, by doing this now Rufus won't connect the restriction with the baby, but as your new rule.

It is very important to make this a rule because no matter how good your baby or how fabulously loving your dog, they should never be left alone in a room together. The gate allows the dog to see into the room to satisfy curiosity and the instinct to protect. Innovative friends of mine found that a screen door worked better for them than a baby gate. Not a bad idea, as the dog had been taught to respect the outside screen door.

Stay away from the suggestion you may have heard to introduce your dog to a baby by carrying a doll around the house. If you play keep-away, the dog will forever try to get at it. And if you lower the doll for the dog to see and sniff (thus supposedly satisfying natural curiosity), the dog will know for sure you are playing games! What dog doesn't know the smell, taste and look of a plastic (cloth or vinyl) toy as opposed to a human being!

There's the danger, too, with this kind of farfetched introduction that the dog may consider the real baby a toy. Whoever thought up this bright idea just didn't know dogs. You can't fool a dog that easily. There's no substitute for the real thing.

HEALTH NOTES

A spayed or neutered dog makes a better pet around kids, so depending on your dog's age, now might be a good time to take care of that. Check with your veterinarian, and while you're at it, be sure

Rufus knows when the gate is up, he can look but not enter.

all immunizations (including rabies vaccine) are current and that the dog is parasite-free. Even when parasites are not found in the first fecal sample, it's wise to check a second time.

H-E-E-E-E-RE'S BABY!

Introduce the dog to the new baby by scent before bringing the baby home. (This scent method, by the way, holds true when adopting a child, too.) The proud Dad (or any other family member) brings home any bit of clothing or receiving blanket that has been on the baby. After greeting the dog and letting Rufus get a good sniff of maternity-room smells on clothing, Dad crouches down to let Rufus sniff the baby-scented article while repeating, "Good dog."

When the baby comes home, let the dog greet Mom first with more sniffing before meeting the newborn. Once that reunion is out of the way, hold the baby down so Rufus can see, sniff and say hello. The dog takes cues from both of you, so it is important for parents to be relaxed about this first meeting.

If you stand up, holding the baby in your arms, the dog will naturally jump up . . . and you will pull away to protect your baby . . . and the dog will jump more frantically . . . and you will panic . . . and . . . well, you get the idea. Don't put yourselves through this torture! Stay calm. Do it the right way.

FIRST SCENT, NOW SOUND

If the baby's cries upset *you*, think what that can do to a dog! Especially one that has never even heard an older child's sobs. Walk, *don't run*, to your screaming infant and let Rufus go with you, casually chatting as you go. Don't say "It's okay"—it's definitely not okay. The screaming may be deafening, and it's probably 3 A.M.! Let your words be more on the order of "Let's go see what's up with Tommy. What is all that noise about!" Rufus won't understand a word of this, but your attitude, tone of voice and body language will get through. Eventually Rufus will connect the word *Tommy* with that small new person in his life.

Maxie gives a smiling okay to the new baby.

Put Rufus on a (much practiced, I hope) Sit-Stay ("Good dog") while you see to the baby. Giving Rufus something to do, like a Sit-Stay or Down-Stay, will help relieve anxiety about the crying. It will indicate to Rufus that *you* are still definitely in charge, that he's part of your team and that the Sit or Down is his job at the moment.

SCENT, SOUND AND SEPARATION

It's a big mistake to keep the dog completely away from the baby. You are all one family and the sooner the dog gets to know the baby is here to stay and what part he or she plays in your lives, the better the dog will figure out its own position and be able to accept it. Include Rufus in your normal daily activities, but time is often a deciding factor in how much undivided attention the dog gets. It pays to have weaned Rufus of indulgences during those months before the baby's arrival.

This is also a very good time to make use of that marvelous piece of dog furniture—the crate! No matter how much you believe in Tinker Bell or Nana the nursemaid dog, crates were made for den-loving dogs and for parental peace of mind. If you must go out of the house or leave the baby even for a minute, take Rufus with you or put him safely in his crate.

NEVER go out of the house and leave baby and dog in a room together with the idea that the dog will baby-sit the infant. This means all the normal, everyday reasons for leaving the house—to put out trash, pick up the mail or newspaper, bring in groceries from the car. Routine stuff, but now you must be aware of where the baby is and where Rufus is. If you go out with the baby in tow, leaving Rufus behind, put him in his crate or close the door to the baby's room. When Mama's away it's often prime time for dear doggy to get into mischief, like emptying diaper pails!

SITTERS

Now you have the baby, no doubt you'll soon be hiring sitters. Whether the sitter is Aunt Minnie, Grandpa or the high-school student next door, the dog has to be considered in your plans. Introduce the person to Rufus and explain where his things are before the sitter's services are required—several times, if possible.

Write down the dog's routine, the veterinarian's phone number, some of the things Rufus knows or does. In other words, *don't* load the sitter down with instructions for little Tommy and then leave the care of Rufus to guesswork. If you do, looking after the dog may be more of a chore and a challenge than caring for your baby. To avoid doggy problems that could interfere with your sitter's care of the baby, your list might look like this:

For Rufus
- Water bowl is next to his crate in laundry room (keep it full).
- Let him outside around 5:30 (check to see gate by garage is latched).
- Feed at 6 P.M.—2 cups kibble, ½ can meat (on counter by his dish).
- Make him say "Please" and put food next to his water bowl.
- Then he sleeps. He barks at back door to go out.
- If he barks outdoors, let him in before he wakes the baby!
- If he gives you any trouble, *smile*, say "Crate!" and give him a biscuit and a toy in the crate.
- Latch the crate door. Can stay up to two hours.
- Vet is Dr. Greenfeld at 555–1234.

BABY ON DOG'S TURF

Training the baby in responsible dog ownership begins when baby Derek joins the four-on-the-floor brigade, which, remember, has been Rufus's exclusive territory until now.

Many a crawler has learned the awkward process of standing, then taking a step or two with the assistance of a tolerant family dog. As baby approaches this stage, set rules to protect both the dog and the baby. A protective dog may take the job of guarding Sara too seriously, in which case keep your cool and be good-natured in relieving the dog of his duties via a simple distraction or even a Time-Out.

An older child can be taught not to pull the dog's hair, ears or tail, not to blow in the dog's nose or try to pry open its mouth, not to

A very good dog!

scream in its ear and so on, but you cannot explain any of these potential hazards to a six-month-old baby or a ten-year-old dog. You are the only one who can envision a possible accident, so you follow two rules: supervise or separate.

On a positive note, you can begin showing Sara how to pet Rufus—"Gently." And award a "good dog" to Rufus for exhibiting tolerance for anything the baby does that warrants it.

PRECAUTIONS

There are little precautions you can take. For example, don't tempt fate. Remove the dog's water bowl and food dish. Even a sweet, docile dog may one day defend its food with teeth. (Feed Rufus when baby naps, or is eating her own dinner in a high chair.) Baby toys are not the dog toys. The reverse is also true. The dog will learn which is which more rapidly than the baby, but then again there's that one day somewhere down the line when they forget. Both baby (through ages

"Goldie wants more, Mom."

three, four or five) and dog (*any* age!) are of a like mind about toys: What's mine is mine, and what's yours is mine if I want it. You'll become the referee. Pick up. Put away. Avoid "No." Small parts of pre-schooler toys are the most dangerous to Rufus, and the most expensive. They usually have to be removed surgically.

Keep soiled diapers where the dog absolutely cannot possibly get at them. You'll regret even a moment's lapse on this rule!

Despite all you may have heard about dogs' mouths being so germ-free as to be almost the perfect cleansing agent, it is pure myth. The saliva in a dog's mouth is as full of bacteria as your own. That's why you don't let Rufus lick the remains of Sara's lunch off her chin or face. If you've always allowed the dog to lick your face, that's your decision, but it's wiser to make baby's face and hands off-limits.

At this stage most of the learning to adapt and change falls on good ol' Rufus, but **as the baby grows, it's the child who must be taught about responsible dog ownership—by instruction, discipline and example**. Now is the time for all members of the family to enforce the rules in similar fashion. No two people are alike in this regard, so consistency is more important than rigid conformity.

BABIES—THE RIGHT AGE?

You don't have a dog, so is this the right time to get one? It is certainly not the optimum time to add a puppy to nursery mayhem (for the reasons already given). An older dog? Maybe.

- IF the dog previously lived with children, was well behaved with babies and young kids.
- IF the dog has had Obedience training (and IF you know how to use it or can find time to attend classes).
- *Any* dog? or do you want a specific look, size, breed, etc?
- IF you previously owned dogs—other than the one you had at age eight that your mother took care of.
- IF you can afford to take on the essential expenses of a pet with a new baby.
- IF you have the time to dedicate to a dog.

- IF you are home all day and IF you intend to remain at home.
- IF you are *not* thinking to return to work leaving a sitter with babe and dog (or worse, dog home alone and baby in day care).
- IF you are not inclined to hypochondria, blaming the dog every time the baby comes down with a sniffle, rash or tummy ache.
- IF all current members of the household can agree to ALL of the above, then . . . maybe.

RIGHT DOG?

An older, trained, laid-back dog with a warm, friendly personality, steady easygoing temperament, large enough to withstand the rigors of a young baby: Is there such an animal? Probably, but perfection is hard to come by and baby Tommy could be in another age group when you have located this paragon of all canine virtues!

Still thinking "maybe"? Okay, then look for as much of the above as you can, and likely breeds include the Collie, Labrador, Golden, Chesapeake Bay or almost any other retriever. Remember that everything sheds—nothing dies with the same hair it's born with. Shorthaired dogs shed—just shorter hairs.

Today almost every breed club has a rescue division, but you would probably be put at the bottom of the list for likely prospective owners. Don't take it personally, but dogs going into a second or third home may have "slight" behavioral problems or for other reasons require a lot of attention.

However, breeders often keep a pup or two they hope will have show or breeding potential. When they don't make the grade, these slightly older dogs (one to two years) go to pet homes. This should be your first choice. Meet the dog, the breeder, at least one parent and perhaps a littermate.

One more IF. *If* possible, take the dog on a trial basis, say for two weeks. Review the situation realistically with the breeder. Listen carefully to all the "ifs" and "what ifs" the breeder has to add. The dog won't suffer any trauma from a brief stay at your house that the breeder can't straighten out. This way, no one, the dog in particular, has to stay in a less-than-good situation.

Goldie adores "her" baby. They share a good laugh.

8

The Toddler and
Pre-Schooler

NOW WE MOVE UP to the toddler stage. If you already have both dog and child, this is the time to be extremely alert to situations where either one could be needlessly hurt. You have two things going for you. As far as the baby is concerned, the dog is just another member of the family; and by now the dog is no longer a little puppy and no doubt adores your baby. An adult dog recognizes the young of any species, so may even tolerate the baby despot to a point, but a puppy is just learning to trust and doesn't need tyrannical surprises.

All of which is to say that toddlers *can* be tyrants. From about eighteen months until around four years of age when they have out-grown it, kids can be mean. It is perfectly normal for this age group to do something mean and nasty now and then because they are testing their boundaries, experimenting with everything in their world. How-ever, someone *must* be around to set limits and put on the brakes.

A good portion of this chapter deals with dog bites, and the intention is not to scare you out of your wits, but simply to prevent serious injury. Dogs do bite—just as they bark, dig and chew. We teach them not to do any of these natural canine activities, which we find inappropriate. Certainly biting tops the list.

Babies put everything that fits (hands, fingers, arms, legs, feet, toes) into their mouths. So do puppies, but "everything" includes people hands, fingers, arms, legs and feet. A pup is taught not to bite, to have a "soft" mouth.

On the other side of this is the child, and here's where we come to the main point of this biting discussion. Parents are responsible for teaching the kids, beginning with baby, how to behave with their own dog as well as with strange dogs, so they will *avoid being bitten*. No matter how much is said about everyday interactions of dogs and kids, requiring supervision, discipline and teaching, the primary goal is always the same: PREVENTION.

SAYING "HELLO"—SAFELY

The first rule of safety is one of awareness. Be aware that *any* dog is capable of biting. And be aware that most dogs do NOT bite, most dogs do like kids and most dogs when approached in a friendly, nonthreatening fashion will respond in the same way. All of which is more significant if you do not yet have a dog and your child's reaction is unpredictable. Since this age span is not the best time to acquire a first dog, much of what follows applies to the toddler or pre-schooler who is not yet a dog owner.

Never let a young child on his/her own approach a strange loose dog. Let me repeat that: NEVER! A toddler, wobbling like a drunken sailor up to a strange dog, could make even a friendly dog feel uncertain or threatened. Naturally unsteady on two feet, a toddler might grab at a tail or ear to steady himself and is likely to be bitten.

When the dog is on-leash, ask the owner for the dog's name and if the dog is friendly with kids. Don't take a yes for more than it's worth. It may mean Bozo likes the owner's son who is eighteen years old, or that he likes the kids next door because they *stay* next door.

Stand still and chat with the owner for a minute or two while you

This child meets a mellow fellow, whose owner wisely is ready to make a quick correction should the dog jump up.

casually assess the dog's reactions to the meeting before going on with the introductions. Look for a happy expression on the dog's face with ears and tail relaxed. Many dogs will sit or become mellow fellows with lowered, slowly wagging tail when approached by very young kids. Give the dog an *A* for sitting on command, too.

Standing over a dog and reaching down to touch it is threatening to a dog, so it's not good manners. Holding the child's hand, crouch down in front of the dog next to your child and put your hand out (palm up) for the dog to sniff. (To be practical, this also puts you in a position to come between dog and child should the need arise.) This body language tells the dog that *you* are friendly and it has nothing to fear. Then hold your child's hand inside yours and let the dog sniff it, too.

Use ordinary good people manners with dogs. For example, dogs don't like to be crowded. Adults don't like it when someone talks right into our faces. Kids don't like it and dogs don't. On the other hand, small children often want to give a big hug to anything soft and fuzzy. Teach little Sara to leave a comfortable, conversational distance between herself and a dog. Any animal that feels trapped or cornered may become fearful, an emotion which can quickly revert to basic animal instinct. When the space to escape has been taken away, the options—as the dog may see it—are attack or be attacked. The difference between the soft, cuddly toy dog and the live version often comes down to teeth!

None of this is meant to scare the living daylights out of you, but if you don't know how a dog looks at the world, it's better to learn some of it here before doing the wrong thing and jumping to the wrong conclusions with young Sara in tow.

IN YOUR FACE

Small children need to be reminded not to put their faces close to the dog's face (I don't care what you may see in those TV commercials that are meant to be cute). *All animals allow each other "flight space"*—a margin of space in which to make a safe and hasty departure should the need arise.

Dogs, like most animals, can feel threatened when this space is violated. The same goes for being stared at. Make your children aware of these things. Ol' Rufus may take all the cuddling, squealing, nose-to-nose and eye contact right in stride, but it may be because he's part of your family and he trusts you all. Not all the dogs you and your kids meet (or a new pup you bring into your home) will necessarily show such tolerance or trust. And Rufus has a boiling point, too.

Children are most often bitten in the face either because of the type of face-off mentioned above, or simply because the child's face is closer to the level of the dog's head. It's why a toddler should not be allowed near the dog's food or water dish, why a young child needs to be taught not to rub noses with a dog or engage in any other face-to-face game the youngster may invent.

The toddler's interaction with a dog requires close supervision for the safety of both baby and pet. Two gentle strokes of a dog's ear may be the prelude to a darn good yank or a pinch. This is invariably what prompts an emergency call to the pediatrician, and while treating

136

a bite wound, the doctor is told, "I don't know why the dog bit her. She was just petting him."

You cannot avoid all accidents, nor can you protect your child from every possible danger. In fact, I believe strongly that my kids learned many important lessons by "doing." A tumble off a swing teaches "hold tight" better than all your speeches. And a small pinch from a dog that's taken enough from a child will get through more clearly than your constant dire warnings.

DOG BITES

This is a rotten subject, so let's get it out of the way!

Dog bites can be avoided by uncomplicated methods. *Prevention* tops the list. Children who are bitten by the family dog are often the instigators of the bite through a lack of basic safety measures. For instance, don't feed the dog while the toddler is toddling about on his/her own or in one of those mobile chairs. Dogs are animals. Animals protect their food. (That's Basic Dog 101.) Feed the dog in the crate while Timmy is eating or when Timmy is napping. Use the dog's water bowl as your object lesson for teaching Timmy not to touch Rufus's dishes. (Saves mopping up, too.)

At this stage, too, it's not only the dog that bites! Child professionals warn parents that it is perfectly normal for toddlers to bite. They also add that the majority of parents generally deny it. Take the information seriously, because *a dog that is bitten will bite back*.

WHY TEETH?

This is possibly the most important section in the book if you have young children. Most dog bites, according to the medical reports, occur in the home. The family dog bites a child. It's essential for kids to understand the differences between their other playmates and their dog.

Even quite small children can understand why a dog uses its mouth and its teeth if you explain (however many times you need to) that the dog doesn't have *hands* to hold things like toys, cookies, Sara's hand, etc., and so it must use its mouth in order to play with Sara (eat her cookies, steal her toys, lead her around the yard)!

On a more serious note, it is interesting how quickly youngsters accept the simple logic of this explanation. By doing so, they also gain a healthier respect for all animals.

TEASING

The problems of squeaking and squealing and quick arm and leg movements are some of the reasons why many breeders are extremely cautious about selling a puppy to families with very young children. Another reason concerns teasing. Siblings are experts at it, offering a cookie or a toy and then snatching it back at the last second. This is Power! And if a sibling isn't around, Rufus is the next best thing. It's just one example of teasing.

Even older children who should know better are apt to wave their hands over the pup's head (read: mouth, teeth) encouraging the puppy to jump up. To the dog, this is a great game, but when the dog does jump up in an attempt to catch what the dog perceives to be pretend prey, invariably it is the DOG that is scolded for jumping up and for snatching, with no explanation given to teach the teasing child. This is why young children should not be allowed to play games like tug-of-war with a dog. It's a fine, fun, very "doggy" game for older kids once they and the dog have been taught how to control it.

Prevent a future disaster. **Correct the one who's doing the teasing, not the one being teased.** Make it a firm family rule: **NEVER tease a dog**. And for very good safety reasons. When a young child puts arms up and waves his/her hands about (with or without toy or treat), where are those hands? Right by the child's face! Now you've got the picture. Need I say more?

JUST A NIP

When a child does get nipped, find out *exactly* what the child was doing and what the dog was doing as it happened. Don't even think of punishing either one! Explain to the child that Rufus was saying, "No,

Sometimes kids plus dog equals chaos!

don't do that.'' Then explain *why* whatever Johnny was doing bothered Rufus.

It is common for the dog to nip at children's legs as they run. That's the clue: *as they run*. Some dogs want to be part of the fun; others are frightened or upset by the activity. Either way, they are apt to use teeth to get a piece of the action. Dogs are naturally predatory animals and chasing quick-moving objects is normal canine behavior. We have taught dogs over the centuries (and still do today) what they may and may not chase, what they may and may not actually catch.

Stephen Budiansky, author of *The Covenant of the Wild—Why Animals Chose Domestication*, in describing the suspension of all dogs in immaturity, points out that they are arrested in one of four stages of juvenile predatory development, with guarding dogs remaining in the first (or fearful) stage, and Border Collies and similar sheepdogs moving on to the third stage of stalking and chasing. He says, ''They will stalk and circle to head off retreating animals, but they usually do not show interest in following through with the kill. Dogs that are arrested in the second stage [playing with objects] include retrievers and poodles.''

Then he notes that Welsh Corgis herd by nipping at the heels of cattle, which puts them in the fourth or final stage, and which also explains why it is pefectly *normal* for these dogs to do the same thing to children. They need to be taught, not punished, so they learn *not* to nip at legs or ankles, particularly those of children. With this natural behavior modified, Corgis make delightful pets and are very good with kids. Dogs of any breed, as well as mixed breeds, can develop this nipping habit. In itself, it's more annoying than dangerous, but needs to be corrected because it *is* annoying and so it does not *become* dangerous.

Apart from teaching Tommy or Sara how to (and how not to) approach animals, teach the dog that's already in your home to accept all kinds of gentle handling, whether it's by the kids, the veterinarian, the groomer or the baby-sitter. Rufus should trust you to look at his teeth, look for burrs or ticks, remove pebbles or road grit from between the pads of his feet. Teach this gentle handling from the day the pup walks in the door.

140

Know how to read typical canine expressions and body posture that may precede a bite. A steady stare is a warning signal. If Bozo does it (Rufus would never!), you can probably turn it off by distraction—"Bozo, Sit," toss a toy and "Fetch it!" However, if it's a strange dog with a hard, steady stare or a curled lip, or growl, take the warnings very seriously. Walk away—sideways if you can. Don't run; dogs give chase instinctively. Above all, do not stare back at the dog.

If your own dog frightens you by anything resembling this type of behavior, don't make excuses and don't delay. Call your veterinarian for the name of a professional who can help.

FINAL WORD ON BITES

Before we leave the subject of bites and nips, no matter how small or large, no matter whether skin is actually broken or not, immediately wash the area thoroughly with soap and warm water. If the dog's teeth only knock against a bone or a tendon, wash the area and then apply ice to prevent swelling. This frequently happens in play and should not be considered a bite, although the kids may tell you it was! It can definitely hurt as much or more than a bite.

JUST A LITTLE SHY

This goes for kids from two to 102! Don't reach out from a standing position to pet a dog that seems shy or frightened. The dog may get behind the owner as you approach, or the owner may say, "Oh, Fluffy is just a little shy." Dogs are shy for a variety of reasons. Some inherit the personality, some are genuinely "just a little shy" and others develop a fear of strangers (or of kids, or of men, etc.) through misguided training. You don't need to know *why* a dog is shy or fearful. Just keep your distance with young Sara, because seemingly sweet, shy dogs are capable of delivering nasty unprovoked nips.

Spot has been given a Time-Out, and Sara is about to have hers!

NOISE

A dog's sense of hearing is acute, and a youngster's shouts of delight or screams of frustration are more penetrating to a dog than to parents. (Oh, I know, but take my word for it.)

There is another kind of noise which a dog that's been raised without children often does not fully understand and therefore reacts inappropriately. For example, little kids squeal, scream, shriek and sometimes explode with the joy of being alive. In response, your dog will probably bark. And bark, and bark!

The mistake that is so often made at this point is to jump on the dog's case, shouting at Rufus to be quiet. This is not the moment for a *No Bark*. Instead, remove Rufus from the scene and calm down the youngsters' noise. If it has gotten out of hand, it's a *perfect* moment for a Time-Out for the kids *and* a Time-Out for Rufus. Emotions are in high gear and everyone's excited. There's nothing whatsoever *wrong* in the kids' behavior. It has simply gotten out of control.

Just remember that the dog's barking is a *response*, not the *cause*.

Remember, too, that a Time-Out is a form of TLC, not a punishment. You might want one yourself!

When a group of children is racing around at play, or solitary Sara gets carried away, don't come down on the dog for wanting to join the fun. But here again, we're up against that mouth (read: hand) and those teeth (read: fingers) in action. (See "Why Teeth?" above) There are lots of times when the kids shouldn't have to stop being kids, so it's wiser to avoid a head-on collision and simply remove the dog from the play area. Don't let punishment even cross your mind. It's separation safety.

When playtime is over, let the kids know that their lively, noisy, squealing activity is okay with *you*, but could cause the dog to grab at them. Impress upon them to remember the rules when you are not around. Remind them again of why the dog uses its teeth: "Look Ma, no hands!"

Dogs, like kids, need to be activated and motivated. They need physical and mental activities to prevent stagnation. And dogs, like kids, will make their own if it's not provided. Parents take heart. One thing you can heave a sigh of relief over: You will never accuse your dog of watching TV all day!

TODDLER AND PRE-SCHOOLER—RIGHT AGE?

Not yet. Plenty of reasons have already been given as to why a toddler or pre-schooler is not a good candidate to own a new dog (puppy or adult). If you don't understand all these explanations for putting the dog idea on hold, you may be upset or even offended when a responsible breeder tells you to come back later—like a year or two later. Your intentions are good. You want a baby puppy as a companion for your baby girl and the pup would certainly add fun and games to your lives, but a puppy (or even an older dog) will require as much or more training, attention and time as baby Sara.

What might be a learning experience for the child, in reality comes down to a question of Mom's time, patience and ability to teach a puppy that's racing in one direction with a shoe in its mouth, while little Sara has toddled off in another to upset the dog's water bowl into the basket of clean laundry! It takes a very special kind of person to

Tiny dogs are not for tiny tots—but perfect for little girls who like to dress up.

pull this off with any degree of success. A saint comes to mind—with the patience of Job.

RIGHT DOG?

If you must, if you yourself simply can't wait another year or so (reread the ''IF'' list in Chapter 7) here are some guidelines.

Generally speaking, large dogs (even giant dogs like Irish Wolfhounds, Great Danes) are better with very little kids than are small dogs. For one thing, they tend to be less active and can take the activity level of this age group without being exhausted or stressed out by it. They are able to tolerate a fair amount of physical contact such as being crawled over, tugged at, plopped down upon, etc. The suggestions given for a baby's dog are also applicable through age five or six.

Tiny dogs are *not* for tiny tots. They conjure up a cute picture, but as mentioned above, little kids fall down, are clumsy and uncoordinated. Little dogs are fragile. Quick. Smart. But fragile.

Feeding Goldie is a serious chore.

9

Older Kids

THE "RIGHT" AGE

A few youngsters may be ready to have a dog at three years of age, others not until five, some not until ten. Studies show that children who have a bond with a companion animal show more maturity than those who don't. Caring for the pet dog increases the development of nurturing qualities in both boys and girls, but this was found to be especially true in the case of little boys of five or six.

THREE TO SIX

Parents must be the judge, but beyond the age of three there is no one truly "right" age. At the younger end of the scale, ages three to six, behavioral changes sometimes occur in youngsters who acquire their first dog, varying from barely perceptible to monumental, from good to bad. This is the child's first role as a parent, which usually means an outpouring of nurturing, caring and loving. The child may take very seriously whatever small duties you assign. Realistically, of course, this sublime state of euphoria won't last. Don't expect too much, just enjoy every minute of it as long as it lasts! Soon after it wears off, you'll no doubt hear yourself mumbling a line every mother/pet owner knows so well, something like: "You didn't feed Star. How would you like it if I forgot to feed you?" My kids had a zillion answers to that one!

A child who harbors resentment for parental authority may take it out on the puppy. A puppy doesn't need a dictator for a friend, so the situation calls for *prompt* adult intervention, patience, Time-Outs and getting the child involved in all the user-friendly aspects of owning a dog. A pup's naturally warm, forgiving attitude helps, too. The result of this could lead to a positive change in the child's attitude when legitimately given the chance to be in charge, but the "boss" needs to be guided into the role of loving caregiver. Not a bad time to teach some good manners, too. To the child, I mean.

NOW I AM SIX

Then there's the only child who has ruled the roost (and the parents) his entire six years of life. He might see his neat little empire going up in smoke, and therefore view the cute, cuddly puppy as a prime target for hostility. On the other hand, this is the type of child who will greatly benefit from sharing and caring for a dog, but there's groundwork to be done first.

Long before getting a puppy, start to explain the changes (the good and the bad) that will take place when the puppy arrives. Some of the good things would be having a pal who won't tell tales or talk back and will keep secrets, teaching the pup tricks, having an in-house playmate and true friend. The down side might include having to pick up toys and clothes, and the whole family having to stick to the puppy's schedule, perhaps getting up a little earlier even on weekends.

Be sure the ground rules are fully understood, because any child who is well organized enough to be the family's CEO will not take kindly to surprises. Appeal to Timmy's managerial skills and enlist his help in caring for the dog wherever possible. A six-year-old can be a

Kids and their dogs making childhood memories.

pretty good dog owner, provided parents recognize a child's limitations and are willing to come to the pup's rescue as needed.

The attitude of parents toward the family dog is the child's best teacher. It's all part of parenting—setting a good example. Very young kids, like puppies, learn much from observation. Both are excellent at sensing the nuances of our feelings or actions.

THE "RIGHT" AGE!

Dogs serve us well in a wide variety of roles, but the one that always stands out is the memory of the dog we had as a kid. Dr. Benjamin Spock noted that the dog was a favorite pet for kids because a dog provides the maximum of nonhuman companionship, is affectionate and brings out warm and tender feelings in the child. Certainly a first-class tribute to the role that the dog plays in a child's life.

All authorities seem to agree that the boy or girl between the ages of seven and ten makes the ideal child custodian of a dog. They are ready and willing to take on some of the responsibility for feeding, grooming, training, exercising with supervision, encouragement and reminders—not nagging!

Acquire a puppy when your youngster is in this age bracket and you pretty much have it made for the next three to four years. These are the golden years when childhood memories are made, memories that will no doubt feature good ol' Star.

A CHILD'S FIRST DOG

Anyone who owns a dog before the first baby is born only has to be concerned with making the appropriate introductions as covered in Chapter 7. The baby will not question or criticize the dog's size, breed, personality or status in the family.

What about the dogless household? Forget the worn-out myth about getting a puppy for your six-month-old baby "so they can grow up together." As you've gathered by now, a baby takes eight to ten years to reach the stage of maturity that a dog achieves in two.

Sharing life with a pet may be the young child's first lesson in kindness and consideration for others. Star may be the only thing that's lower on the social scale for the pre-schooler to manipulate, and there's nothing more manipulative than a youngster (except maybe a dog!). Here is the perfect opportunity to teach such abstracts as the give-and-get of friendship and generosity.

The older pre-schooler is now taught not to upset the dog's water bowl, not because it makes a mess, but because it would deprive Star of a much-needed drink. Sara learns to leave the sleeping dog alone, not because it might bite her, but out of consideration for others. Six-year-old Timmy learns not to yell or hit the dog when it grabs the baseball, but to say, "Sit, good dog. Give it, good dog." So Timmy begins to understand through action the concept that civilized behavior brings quicker, more satisfactory results than the use of force.

But the kids in that "perfect" age bracket are in prime time for dog ownership. They take pride in ownership, pride in teaching the dog everything from balancing a treat on its nose, to retrieving whatever is thrown, to catching a Soft Bite Floppy Disc (a great toy for dogs

Timmy learning how to get his baseball back. (Both dog and boy still showing a little of the yes-you-will, no-I-won't phase.)

and safe for very young kids as well as young puppies). The older the children, the more responsibility they can undertake (thankfully!) in the daily care of Star.

There is a difference in selecting a dog as a pet for an only child or one that is meant to entertain or occupy several young children. One child, one dog is apt to be highly successful, whereas the dog entering a large family can run into a few problems that are worth noting. For example, the dog may become the center of controversy. When she behaves, she's mine; misbehaves, she's yours; needs to go out, she's yours; wants to play, she's mine.

It's more serious if the dog is confused by rules or commands that are not the same from each child. This is the cause of a high incidence of behavioral problems. Again, we're back to family planning, family training and family agreement to maintain consistency in life with the dog. For some kids who can't agree with each other on anything, this can be a difficult goal, but dogs are resilient and this is an excellent learning experience.

Getting a dog for a child is a family affair. The more they are encouraged to participate in the preliminary discussions of which breed, what their responsibilities will be, why they want a pup, etc., the more they'll learn and the better prepared they'll be to continue to care for the dog when the shine wears off and they're down to ho-hum everyday life.

HIM? OR HER?

Decide, too, the pros and cons of male or female. Only thirty years ago children's books were completely dominated by boys because male dominance was accepted. What's more, via the text in schoolbooks as well as illustrations, the Freudian concept of "boys do; girls are" was actually taught. While this has never been the case with dogs, some people are rigid in "We only want a male," or "We're only interested in a female," for no particular reason, or worse, for some unfounded one.

In certain breeds, the males are "more dog" (stronger and larger, with personalities to match) but this does not by any means preclude their being the right choice for kids. Please don't fall for the bit about bitches being better (i.e., more motherly) with children. There is nothing in the "Book According to Dog" (that's the one the dogs go by) that says a female is going to be a nursemaid or surrogate mother to your child, or even like kids more than a male would. That's fantasy. Think about it: Where did the adjective *bitchy* originate?

If you're worried about a lifted leg on shrubs, there are numerous safe repellents on the market. A properly housetrained male will not lift his leg indoors anymore than a female would squat. A neutered male won't "mark territory" (that is, leave two drops here, there and everywhere). See the adults of the breed and ask several breeders what differences they have observed.

Then, when you've made your decision, ask the breeder (and double-check with your veterinarian) about the best age to have the male neutered or the female spayed. This is for the health of your dog; it eliminates 95 percent of gender-related cancers; it contributes to modifying behavior (less marking of territory) and of course prevents any further rise in the population of unwanted, unhomed, unloved pets, which is another aspect of responsible dog ownership to teach the kids about. If you want your kids to learn about reproduction and birth, teach it at home, or there are books in your library and it is taught in school.

A DOG IS FOR LIFE

"A Dog Is for Life, Not Just for Christmas" is a theme being used by the American Kennel Club in an effort to make people realize that buying or adopting a dog is an eight to fifteen year commitment, not just a passing fancy. In our throwaway society, we are beginning to see the light. "A dog is for life" means the life cycle of the dog, *not* until our lifestyle changes, or the dog is no longer cute, or we're too busy or too tired to groom it or walk it. Responsible dog ownership begins with educating the children.

Kids start by learning that a puppy is not a toy. It must not be squeezed, tugged, tossed, pulled or dragged around. Things that physically hurt a child also hurt the dog—hitting, pinching, poking, pulling hair.

153

Star can't be stuck in the toy box when playtime is over. Every day, no matter what else is going on, the dog must be fed, watered, exercised and given friendly companionship. She must be taught good manners at home and basic Obedience in school for her own safety and welfare as well as ours and to conform to society. Once a week Star must be groomed and at least once a week given a special walk or extra playtime. Twice a year she needs preventive veterinary care. Don't leave the kids at home. It's good for them to know Star's doctor—and they'll take a fiendish delight in seeing someone else getting a shot!

What's in it for the family? In return, you and the kids get a 100 percent noncritical companion 365 days a year, a warm security blanket when life isn't so great, a partner who doesn't complain when dinner is late or smells like leftovers, a friend who looks at you adoringly every day whether or not you deserve such adulation . . .

(Feel free to fill in the rest of the paragraph!)

NOW OR LATER

Kids often beg for a puppy, and with every good intention in the world promise to love, honor, cherish—and teach it to obey! But all their good intentions go out the window the day soccer practice begins, or there's too much homework, or when a dozen other normal childhood activities interfere with their original assurances.

Parents need to be just as realistic as they would like their offspring to be. If your kids are at that age when wanting a puppy is just today's "want," explain the depth of such a commitment in only as much detail as may be necessary, ending up by saying firmly, "Definitely not now, but let's talk about it." And keep your promise.

Then if the desire for a dog is genuine, long-term and at least somewhat plausible, and *if* you are prepared to take over where your child can't (see above), and *if* everything else in your life indicates that it is the right time to get a puppy, put together a practical, very flexible schedule your child will be able to follow successfully.

Just don't set the kids up for inevitable failure. Don't give sleepyhead Tommy the job of taking the puppy outside first thing in the morning. The pup will mess in her crate before he gets to her and you'll be upset with both of them. What's worse, Tommy will have been a failure. There will be lots of times when you will have to lead the way or take over. Be prepared to do it graciously, without recrimination (even if this means *you* have to take a Time-Out!). Sometimes, work out a fair exchange. You'll feed the dog so Tommy won't be late for practice, and he'll do some small chore for you.

There is one more thing to be prepared for. Should the dog not work out, for whatever reason, take plenty of time to explain to the children that it was not their fault. Even if you harbor the tiniest suspicion that it was, do not let the kids get even a whiff of it. You may have to repeat over and over again the various reasons why it didn't work. So be it. If the dog somehow does not fit into your family unit, no child should ever be allowed to feel he or she is a failure at pet ownership. If at all possible, deal with what went wrong and start again.

THE CHOICE

Be superrealistic in selecting a breed that's right for your kids. This is not the time to be swayed by a dog on a TV commercial. If you're in a small apartment, hoping to move to a house next year, now is not the time to get a Siberian Husky. Wait until next year. Most breeds of dogs are good with kids, but there are many of the same differences among dogs as are seen in the kids. Some are very active, others a bit aloof, some too large, some too small, some more (some less) prone to stir up allergies. Go to dog shows, puppy matches, visit breeders, ask questions.

LOOK AT ADULTS

Learn what to expect beyond those first few weeks when all puppies are adorable. Observe your child's interaction with the puppies and with the adult dogs, keeping in mind that an adult dog of almost any breed, not regularly exposed to children, may come on strong—

especially kenneled stud dogs. Young children may be enchanted with the serious, teddy-bear look of Rottweiler puppies, but be totally unprepared for the size and strength of the adult dogs. The same goes for any breed. You don't really want your child to fall in love with a Sheltie pup on the mistaken assumption that it will grow up to be a Collie!

It's imperative to meet the adults of the breed. This is one reason a pet shop is not always a wise place to go for a child's first dog. Nearly two-thirds of all puppies acquired as children's pets are given away or turned over to shelters within the first year simply because their cuteness, cuddliness or just plain "puppyishness" wore off and their owners were not prepared for the adult dog and adult dog behavior. Since this generally means euthanasia, it's sad for the innocent puppy, but worse, the throwaway mentality is perpetuated and gives the kids a double whammy: Sensitive children may feel it is all their fault. Others perceive it as an example set by their parents that life has little or no value.

Do your homework, take your time and choose a breed that suits your kids, your home, your finances and your family lifestyle (the latter, as far as you can guess for the next ten to twelve years!). There are over three hundred different breeds in the world, but most people freely admit to being swayed by "something about" two or three. Often it is the looks of the dog that we fall for. However, dogs are grouped by the work they were originally bred to do, not by the length of their ears and tails, or by their pretty faces.

Hounds were bred to hunt by sight or scent, sporting breeds to hunt with people or alone (some on land, others in water); herding dogs are tireless workers bred to herd all movable objects (including kids and cats); terriers are active dogs bred to be quick and to enjoy chasing vermin (and kids and cats); working breeds got the tough jobs like pulling sleds or guarding property. And then there are small Toy breeds (the original pampered pets) held in arms or laps it is said to keep fleas off their owners!

This is obviously a very general overview, but knowing what a breed is genetically engineered to do will give you insight into what you can expect in the way of temperament and activity level. *Bear in mind that almost any puppy becomes the dog you make it.*

156

STAR IS HERE! NOW WHAT?

What can little kids do? A very young child (with a reasonably well-trained dog) can have the dog sit before putting down her dinner. The same youngster could help prepare the dinner with the aid of a stool at the kitchen sink. Kids of this age love slopping in warm soapy water, so what better job than washing the dog's dish and water bowl?

They *can* help in the daily care of their dog. *What* they can do will depend upon their individual manual dexterity, upon their size and strength and, to a large extent, upon parental patience and good-natured encouragement. Ask a five-year-old to refill the dog's water bowl and stand by with the mop! But encourage the effort, praise whatever portion of the venture you can. Phoney admiration is worse than none. Kids know when they've goofed and you are faking the praise. They notice, too, that Star is only praised or rewarded for doing something right. False praise is not good for dogs either.

Here's one way to let a small child fill a water bowl. A one-quarter-filled bowl is difficult enough to carry and put down, so let that be the goal. (Keep the mop handy anyway.) Then let Derek add more water from a plastic bottle with a handle.

Now take a look at what you've accomplished: a little boy who can put down water for his dog, can fill a bottle, carry it to the water bowl and pour it in. Some days he can even do it without spilling any!

Think ahead: Stainless steel or solid plastic bowls make a terrible racket when dropped, but they don't break! Save the fancy crockery with the dog's name for later. For little kids, play it safe.

Here is a tip on how to let a small child offer any dog a treat. Put the treat on the child's open hand, supported by yours underneath. Your hand is there, so the dog knows it's okay but gets the scent of the child's hand, too. Holding the treat flat on the open palm, fingers together, will save small fingers from being pinched if a large dog snatches its treat too quickly. Dogs recognize adults as authority figures and kids as littermates. By standing behind the child, you are literally ''backing up'' the child's new role.

Lucky kids to have found family training classes.

SCHOOL DAYS

School-age children can do loads of things with their dogs, depending to some extent upon where they live and in certain cases upon the actual age and ability of child and dog.

Let's say the puppy is between ten weeks and five months of age; you can begin with KPT, or Kindergarten Puppy Training. If Star is older than that (even a lot older), you'll start regular Obedience classes. Plan to attend at least two sessions without Star to see how the classes are run, if you all like the instructor, whether or not there's a good mix of sizes of dogs and ages of people. A young child with a Scottie puppy would be mentally and physically undone in a class of adults with Dobermans and Newfoundlands.

It's a pity so few trainers offer classes especially for children or families. Ask around. You may be lucky and find one in your area. Training the dog to be an obedient and well-mannered member of the family requires each person in the family to understand what the dog is being taught and how. It is important for the whole family to get

158

into the act, and family classes are a much-needed solution on both the parental and the offspring levels.

But if your area contains only traditional classes (one owner/handler to one dog), then at least try to locate classes that do not have competition as their only goal. You need to be taught ways to motivate your dog to be good at home and away, with the kids, the sitter and Grandma.

You don't expect ten-year-old Tommy to make sharp physical corrections on a dog that outweighs him by fifteen pounds. So what if Star does a "sloppy Sit"! If her tail is wagging and Tommy is giggling at their success, that's all that counts. Dogs are very easy to train; children are easy because they listen, they watch and they're game to try. Teaching adults is hard because they're full of inhibitions, or they know it all, or they don't know right from left. That's probably why there are so few family classes.

If, on the other hand, Dad has trained the dog and wants young Jason to learn, all three should work as a team. The dog will respect Jason's command to heel if Dad is holding the lead and Jason is in the middle gently holding the slack. As Dad moves and signals the dog, Jason will learn how to use the lead. Dad is there to show Star that this new turn of events is okay. Trust and respect can't be overemphasized.

The basics—Heel, Sit, Come, Down, Stay and Stand—are taught in the Beginners' class. That's what (you hope) the dog will learn. What you learn will be the footwork (dogs read body language), coordination, timing, how to use your voice and how to show the dog what you mean by those basic commands. These are great skills for kids to acquire, and as in sports, there's the flush of success, the agony of defeat. Good learning experiences, and the best part is Star doesn't criticize or complain.

Sessions are once a week for six or eight weeks. If you practice and your dog is doing well, you can then go on to a Pre-Novice class. Be prepared to repeat this one a couple of times before you are both ready for the next class (Novice), where you'll be working the dog on those same commands, but off-lead. Now you're into big-time stuff that can take you right into the Obedience Trial show ring!

No matter how far beyond the first two sessions the child and Star go or don't go, they will have had fun together and learned a lot about each other, and the dog will have some basic good manners on which to build. Trainers often suggest practicing "for ten minutes, twice a day."

That's okay, but a much better way is to practice any time Star is awake just by using all the things she has learned. Good manners are only as good as they are practiced. Going to the next room? It's "Star, Heel." Through a door? "Star, Sit." You go through, and then, "Star, Come." Greeting Aunt Em at the front door? "Star, Stand-Stay." "Sit, shake hands." "Down, roll over." This stuff is only limited by your child's imagination!

Of course, anyone who gets bitten by the Obedience bug can continue with more instruction and more challenges. But with basic Obedience, the child and Rufus are now ready for all kinds of other exciting activities.

10

The Family:
Changes in Lifestyle

THE CLOSER THE DOG is to one person in the family (typically, the spoiled dog or child substitute), the less able the dog is to cope with the stress of changes in lifestyle. This is true regardless of the extent of the change. Some dogs are so neurotic about their owners, they can't even manage a switch in work hours, let alone the stress of a prolonged separation. If you're saying to yourself, "Yes, that's my Leo," for your dog's sake reread the section on weaning a dog of your undivided attention. No one's life is stuck in a permanent groove, and Leo will be a far happier dog if he can adapt.

FAMILY VACATIONS

If you're a dog owner, there are only two kinds of vacations: those with the dog, and those without the dog. Let's Go!

Taking Rufus along on a family vacation requires some planning

The "perfect" family—each kid has a dog.

in order to be the success you have in mind. First, the dog must enjoy riding in the car. Carsick dogs do not make for happy holidays. Secondly, check with your vet to be sure all the dog's immunizations, including rabies vaccine, are current. Packing for the dog is a bit like packing for a little kid, but thankfully without the usual begging to take along twenty-four dolls or a collection of spacemen!

What to pack for the dog includes:

1. Crate, or car barrier and/or seat belt or harness
2. Food dish and water bowl
3. Enough water from home to last at least part of your trip (or buy bottled)
4. A supply of food (a fork to mix kibble and canned, and a can opener!); treats. Generous supply of any needed medication. Changes in water and/or food commonly cause tummy upsets in dogs, which takes you right back to that first thing I mentioned.
5. Brush, comb and flea and tick spray

6. Several large dog towels. Wet or muddy dogs are not pleasant companions in close quarters.
7. Dog collar—Check very carefully to be sure the collar fits and has no worn areas that might break. Do NOT travel with a choke-chain training collar on the dog. Rufus's ID and rabies tags are a must and they belong on a buckle collar (seat-belt-type buckles are fine).
8. Leash—Check that the leash is strong, including the snap and the hand loop. Take along an extra collar and an extra leash that allows the dog greater freedom. The retractable kind is perfect because it gives Rufus a twenty to thirty foot radius for sniffing and otherwise enjoying good exercise, while you amble on at your own rate but maintain full control.

In warm weather be prepared either to leave Rufus crated in the car, parked in the shade with all windows open, or take him with you. **Heat exhaustion strikes quickly**.

If you are unsure how your dog will react to other people and dogs, for example in a campground, you might want to play it safe by

Rufus is ready to go. Where are the kids?

using a head halter, or even a lightweight muzzle. Another case of better safe than sorry and sued.

The kids need to know that dogs are easily disoriented away from home. Every summer, vacationing dogs get lost because people think Rufus will behave off-lead in strange surroundings just the way he does at home.

Kids generally burst out of cars upon reaching their destination (or a pit stop), or out of motel rooms to reach the pool or playground. Teach them to check on Rufus first. Losing a dog hundreds of miles from home is a horrible way to end a holiday. You've been practicing the "Wait" Obedience command. Use it now while you snap on the leash. Don't rely on "Rufus, come" when you're on unfamiliar turf.

On the theory that preparing for the worst prevents it from happening, stick a clear close-up picture of Rufus in the glove compartment, together with a copy of the rabies certificate, your vet's name and the name of a neighbor who can be reached while you are away—just in case Rufus takes an illegal walk.

If you are visiting family or friends, abide by house rules regarding where Rufus sleeps, eliminates, stays during meals or a picnic, etc. Resident dogs and cats, gerbils, hamsters, et al., have primary rights. Visiting pets do not have guest privileges! When in doubt, Rufus should be in that ubiquitous crate.

A HAPPY CAMPER STAYS BEHIND

There are several ways to leave Rufus behind when you go off on vacation. Good old Aunt Em or your next-door neighbor of course is great, but a newer type of day care is the bonded professional dog sitter who comes to your home as many times a day as you choose to exercise, feed, water and play with a lonely Rufus.

Then there are boarding kennels. These facilities vary in type, size and quality, running pretty much the same gamut as our own inns and motels. The dice are somewhat loaded in favor of the kennel operator, because Rufus can't tell you what was wrong with the place, so before making a reservation, inspect the premises—even if it's where your best friend leaves Spunky.

Call ahead to make an appointment to see the facility. Ask the same questions you'd ask of a nursery school or kids' camp. Ask to see where the dogs are housed and exercised, what they are fed, what the charges are including the extras. If you see a certificate from the American Boarding Kennel Association (ABKA) on the wall, it means the kennel passes the rigid requirements of that national organization. Use your nose to tell you how clean the place is. A heavy odor of disinfectant or bleach on your inspection tour is good, whereas a heavy scent of potpourri may be only a cover-up. Just don't expect it to smell like home.

Many boarding kennels put the dogs in crates for some portion of the day or night. Smart you, to have crate-trained Rufus long ago so he'll be completely relaxed in his temporary home.

Plan to drop the dog off in the morning so all day can be spent getting to know the staff, the other "guests," the routine, and by bedtime Rufus will be ready to settle down for a night's sleep.

THE LOST DOG

A lost dog is a real heartbreak for any kid. The child goes through many of the same emotional reactions when the dog is lost as when a dog dies. Anger—why did Rufus do this to me when I was so good to him? Guilt—if I hadn't yelled at him (or if I had remembered to walk him, etc.), he wouldn't have run away. And bargaining—if you come back, I'll never yell at you again. And so on. Or perhaps a child just relates more closely with the feelings of being lost.

Positive steps begin with *prevention*.

1. Get Rufus tattooed and registered with an organization such as the National Dog Registry.
2. Keep fences in good repair.
3. Buy a new collar and leash before the old ones show signs of wear.
4. Teach the dog "Wait" and to not go through any outside door until you say so.
5. Teach the kids as much about safety as they can take!

But, let's say at some point, for whatever reason, Rufus takes a walk on his own. The first thing to do is take a leash, a handful of dog biscuits or other treats and, calling his name, walk in the direction anyone saw him go, or take your normal route. Dogs are creatures of habit. Do NOT drive around in the car calling the dog. By the time the dog hears you (and hopefully runs to meet you), you'll be a mile away.

Alert all delivery people on your street, as well as all the neighbors. Ask everyone to crouch down, to call the dog by name and *if* Rufus comes, to KEEP HIM SAFE until you can get there! (Be thankful you socialized Rufus so he likes people.) If you're alone, get a friend to stay by your phone. Tell all the kids in your neighborhood and offer a reward. Young kids, by the way, are great at finding dogs because most family pets just naturally gravitate toward groups of youngsters.

A word on rewards. Large cash rewards occasionally trigger an outbreak of stolen dogs, especially when advertised in a local paper. It's better to state ''Reward'' without mentioning an exact sum. Kids, for example, might be happier with a group reward. Take them to McDonald's or an amusement park.

If Rufus is gone for more than just a few hours without a trace, it's time to get into high gear.

1. Call the animal control officer in your town and in all surrounding towns (dogs don't read road signs).
2. Call all shelters, again in your town and all surrounding ones.
3. Call your local radio station if they regularly announce missing pets (most small towns do).
4. Put up posters wherever possible, but be sure they can be read by someone sitting in a car. Use a broad marking pen and give a brief, accurate description of the dog and a telephone number. For example:

MISSING

''RUFUS''

BLACK LAB, MALE

RED COLLAR, ID, LICENSE TAGS

555-6000 (DAY)

555-4422 (EVE)

5. Good, clear snapshots can be added to posters for store windows or bulletin boards, libraries, school bus stops, etc.

If the dog is reported as having been seen, go there and stay awhile. Leaving behind an old piece of your clothing (with a dog biscuit tucked inside) will impart your scent in that area in case Rufus returns. Ask people there to be on the lookout and to call you if they see him again.

The quicker you are in spreading the word, and the wider you spread it, the better your chances are of getting the dog back safe and sound.

A friend of mine left her kitchen door open overnight, and sure enough, at her normal wake-up hour of 6 A.M., the dog trotted back into the house as casually as you please!

Regardless of how long the dog has been gone, what anguish you've been through and how much trouble it has caused, when you finally see Rufus coming toward you (or go to pick him up at the dog pound) BE OVERJOYED in your welcoming him back into your life!

DIVORCE STATISTICS

Some separations are not happy events for anyone, including the dog, and in some cases, especially for the dog. A breakup of the family unit is one of those times. Statistics indicate that almost half of all marriages in the United States end up in divorce, and it is estimated that more than half of unmarried couples also split up.

Dogs do not seek divorce, but their statistics often reflect the outcome of divorce, with the dogs ending up in shelters as "unwanted." Not only are they unwanted and casually discarded, but dogs are emotional victims of divorce.

A growing field in child psychology deals with ways of explaining to children that their parents' divorce is not the kids' fault. Just try explaining that to a dog! So Rufus gets thrown out at the precise time when "his" children as well as one or more adult owners are most likely to need a best friend in the truest sense of the word. Taking a dog for a walk and chewing his ear off with your problems is great therapy.

THE "FAMILY" DOG?

In speaking to numerous divorce lawyers, family counselors, child psychiatrists and others concerned with aiding all those involved in the breakup of the family, not *one* had ever even considered the dog as a part of that family. It's particularly bewildering in view of the fact that there is complete acceptance among many of these same professionals of the therapeutic benefits of the human/animal bond.

The reasons given for regarding the dog as less important than who gets the VCR are all purely monetary. A Picasso and a fancy sportscar all have a distinct cash value, something worth fighting for. The legal view of divorce is purely a division of a couple's financial holdings. The dog is expendable. Unless brought to the marriage by either one of the couple and so claimed by prior ownership, Rufus is apt to be viewed now as excess baggage, another nuisance to have to deal with, even though much thought and deliberation may have gone into his acquisition.

If this weren't enough, the children, thrust into an adult world of conflict, are not even asked about their feelings for their dog. The only questions lawyers (and sometimes, parents) ask children are: "Do you want to live with Mommy or Daddy?" and "How often would you like to visit [the other parent]?" Family counselors and child psychologists are primarily interested in whether or not the children feel the divorce was their fault.

These are certainly important things to discuss, but a dog often figures right up there, just as prominently, in the hearts of the kids. But no one asks.

A Boy and His Dog

It was a young boy's statement about his dog that started my research into the entwined lives of dogs and kids—and the impact of divorce. "My mother got me, and my father got my dog," he said with heartbreaking simplicity. He visited his dog (and his father, as required by court order), but the boy and his dog were grieving over *their* separation.

The dog was misbehaving as never before. The boy had literally

A boy and his dog with Dad. Now everything is okay.

lost his best friend and was miserable. When it was pointed out to the father what was wrong, and when he understood that the emotional problems were caused by the split, a good solution was worked out whereby the dog and his boy saw more of each other.

The dog actually became the catalyst for father and son. Instead of museum tours and fast-food meals that neither of them enjoyed, and where the conversation was stilted and awkward, their activities switched to hiking, camp-outs, fishing—things they had never done together before—and all because these were adventures in which they could include the dog.

The Canine Therapist

Parents, as well as those counseling the family, will find it easier in a family crisis to get through to children via the family pet. A dog is a silent partner for a child, a trusted confidant, a warm furry security blanket to hold onto or cry into. *Where will I live? What will my friends say? Where will I go to school? Can I still love Dad if Mom doesn't?*

The dog listens, really listens (not the way parents often do with one ear on something else), and the dog tacitly agrees, is never critical—and NEVER tells! For a child going through the emotional upheaval of a divorce, there is probably no better therapist than his or her dog. When kids and dogs bond, according to the dog, it's for life.

A devoted dog can help young children (three to six years): by providing some semblance of continuity of the family unit; by easing the fear of abandonment; by accepting regressive behavior such as thumb-sucking, crying or bed-wetting without any comment whatsoever.

For older children of seven or eight, the dog provides constant and consistent companionship; a friend to share tears of anger and grief; a feeling of "we" and "us" when all the normal attempts by the child to reconcile the parents fail; an audience to share hostile feelings about parents' dates; a genuine possession and so a sense of pride in ownership.

Older teenagers tend to look at divorce with an attitude of "How could you do this to me?" (resentment, shame and a growing mistrust of their own relationships). However, the nine-to-twelve age group

Older kids have very personal views when their parents divorce.

experiences the same fear of abandonment as the younger children, but is also into laying on the guilt and heavily criticizing their parents. There's also worry about the future (school, home, friends). Again, the dog is perceived by these kids as the stabilizing faction in their lives.

If nine-year-old Johnny decides to run away from home (actually, from the situation at home), the chances are he'll take Rufus along—misery likes company—and the whole escapade may end up being a long walk until dinnertime. And that in itself, "Rufus wanted his dinner," is a plausible reason for Johnny to return home. It's a valid, adult-sounding explanation.

Custody, Joint or Otherwise

A child who hears "the house is mine" or "the car is yours" should at least be allowed the dignity of being able to say "Rufus is mine!" It's a small way for parents to boost their own image in the child's eyes to let the child possess something of value.

When joint custody of the children is in a divorce settlement (something recently determined to have a lasting debilitating effect on kids), it might help the children if the family pet moved back and forth, too. However, this arrangement could easily backfire. A dog brought into the home by one parent might then only serve as a bitter reminder to the other.

When there are no children involved, shared custody of the dog does not usually last. One or the other person decides to get a dog of his or her very own and relinquishes interest in the original pet. There's always the chance, too, that the dog won't go for this new shared lifestyle. Stress shows up as poor behavior or even a change in temperament, not unlike the way a young child acts up in a similar situation.

A Legal Solution

One lawyer put her finger on an area of conflict and came up with a possible solution. She suggested fair compensation for the upkeep of the dog be awarded the mother when given custody of the children. It is normal now for such a single mother to continue (or return) to work and therefore the dog might be seen as an extra financial burden. However, a woman in this predicament would be more likely to consider keeping Rufus for his therapeutic and guardian value to the kids if the ex-husband were to contribute toward the dog's expenses. This view might have added legal appeal for both sides, too, if the children of the divorce are to become latchkey kids.

TWO'S COMPANY OR CONFLICT?

Dogs are sometimes confronted with the fact that their owner is about to team up with another partner who owns (oh yes, dear Rufus!) another d-o-g. This can be four-way happiness or a highway collision.

Let the dogs meet and get to know each other on neutral turf. Go for walks anywhere so long as it's away from either home. Keep both dogs on-leash. After a few introductory jaunts have worked out satisfactorily, bring along the kids (his and/or hers) but don't let them come on strong at first. Smothering a dog with loving hugs to impress a parent won't work. Dogs don't like to be overwhelmed, but if everyone plays it cool, dogs are generally good at this game of "your kids, my kids, our kids" and take it all in stride.

If not, brush up on straight basic classroom Obedience with both dogs while they're together. Switch dogs every now and then so they can work with both partners and learn this is indeed a family affair. Just please don't assume they will love each other on sight as much as you two people love each other, or even as much as you each like your own dog. It may help if you think of the two dogs as in-laws, not siblings!

SORRY, WE CANNOT KEEP THE DOG

Not everything in life is perfect, and there are circumstances that make it impossible to keep Rufus, even for the sake of children. Explain to your kids in terms they can easily understand and answer as best you can the question why (how, when and where) you must part with Rufus.

How you handle this decision can have a lasting effect on the children, but there are valid reasons. For example, you may be moving from a house with a backyard to a high rise in the city where the dog would have to be walked last thing at night on not-so-safe streets. Or perhaps you are moving back in with parents and Grandpa has two dogs who will not tolerate yours.

Just be sure to tell the truth. A young woman told me of her feelings about her dog's fate. She was a child when her parents divorced. She was told her dog was with friends and was fine. Thousands of miles away, the little girl missed her dog terribly. Many years later she stumbled upon the truth.

Her dog had suffered greatly from the stress of separation, refusing to eat, howling for hours on end, biting those who offered help, and so was shuffled from one person to another until someone thoughtfully had the dog put to sleep. Twenty years later, this grown woman can accept the divorce that disrupted her life, but cannot bring herself to forgive those who lied to her about the well-being of her best friend.

If the dog was a loving, living gift from one member of the couple to the other, the decision is a tough one. *Think first, last and only of what will be best for the dog.* Giving the dog to Mom and Dad won't work if Mom and Dad are not just dying to have the dog! It won't work either if they are under the mistaken impression that this is a temporary measure. The same goes for your best friend, your good friends or your wonderful neighbors.

When this type of arrangement is the best you can do, write up an agreement (even with your own dear old Dad!) stating who pays for vet bills, food, grooming, license, toys. List the brand names of dog food, quantities fed and at what time. List some of the words the dog knows. And—underline this—spell out exactly what is to be done if this person cannot keep Rufus. Each of you sign both copies and each keep a copy. Better safe than sorry and sued later. Even close families can get into court battles over seemingly simple things.

BREED RESCUE

You may be in luck if you purchased the dog from a breeder. Most breeders today are associated with breed rescue, or can put you

174

in touch with someone. These people are dedicated to finding not just a new home, but the "right" home for every dog of their breed in need. Health and temperament are evaluated, previous home life and age considered before placing the dog. Follow-up guidance is assured.

Regardless of where Rufus goes next, plenty of TLC as well as retraining to a new routine will be needed. When to get up, when to eat, when to go out, when to go to bed! No two households are alike, so be sure the next home knows what the previous basic routine has been. Add any little things that might help should Rufus seem confused or homesick. Sending a dog off, whether for a couple of days or for life, with an old article of your clothing (a sock or T-shirt) helps bridge the sense of loss. Sometimes a dog appears to fit right into a new home and then falls apart. It's a dog's way of telling you it's been nice visiting, but now it's time to go home. Extra fun-filled walks are excellent therapy for a homesick dog.

UNPLACEABLE

It may be especially hard to place the dog because he is old. Not too many homes welcome someone else's aged dog, so if Rufus is having trouble seeing or hearing, or requires a special diet or medication, or suffers from arthritis or incontinence, *please consider euthanasia*. Not casually dropped off at the local shelter, but taken to your own veterinarian with whom you can discuss it and get answers to your questions.

This suggestion is also valid for a dog you know has a behavioral problem few others would put up with, especially if there is the possibility of danger. For instance, if the dog is aggressive with strangers, or is difficult to control on-leash, or is not good with children, or just has a short wick and is therefore not reliable. You cannot in good conscience pass along to an unsuspecting family a potentially dangerous dog masquerading as a pet.

Whatever your decision, be sure your children understand exactly what the future holds for their Rufus, explaining gently why it is not possible to keep him. And if you decide that euthanasia is the kindest thing for your dog, please read the section "Explaining the Death of a Pet."

TEMPORARY GOODBYES

There are other, less dramatic separations. Baby Sara grows up and goes to school all day. Mom goes back to work maybe part-time at first, then full-time. Young Timmy goes off to college. Even if Rufus by now has become a canine senior citizen, the shared activities and physical presence of these family members will be missed. A few special treats like a new interactive toy, favorite walks, a little leniency in the house rules, food treats (healthy ones like yogurt, carrots, apple) all will go a very long way toward letting Rufus know HE is still "family."

CARE OF THE OLD DOG

About 41 percent of dogs in the United States are considered geriatric—a direct reflection on our improved general health and the nutritional care of our dogs. But as dogs live longer, more dog owners are in need of information on their care.

It's a difficult to explain canine old age to Kimmy. Rufus is her best friend.

An old dog may need special care that isn't easy to explain to a young child. Sometimes physical comparisons can be made to grandparents. For example, the dog can't see, but dogs can't wear glasses like Grannie does. Rufus can't hear, and ditto regarding hearing aids. He can't race around the house anymore, and Grannie has arthritis, too. He sleeps a *lot* more—so does Grandpa.

Dogs become senior citizens at different ages depending somewhat upon their breed or actual size. The American Animal Hospital Association published the following chart as a general guide. Dogs are individuals, but this is when the average dog enters old age:

Size	Age
Small Dogs (under 20 lbs.)	11 years
Medium Dogs (21–50 lbs.)	10 years
Large Dogs (51–90 lbs.)	9 years
Giant Dogs (over 90 lbs.)	7 years

The old dog needs extra care—protection from weather (hot or cold, wet or windy) and from the artificial sources such as heaters and air conditioners. The dog may be less agile and unable to get out of the way of active children, nor as able to keep up with the kids. He may want to keep up, and tries, but you must be the judge of whether or not he is physically able to do whatever he wants.

Rufus's hearing and sight will probably diminish, so the family may eventually become his eyes and ears. Deafness is just one reason old dogs do not like being disturbed; it startles the dog and he reacts with a snap or a snarl. Approach the deaf dog by stamping your foot (he'll get the vibrations). For the blind dog, leave furniture just as it is and he'll navigate fine. Kids need to be told about these changes taking place between life and death.

EXPLAINING THE DEATH OF A PET

Death is a difficult subject for most of us to talk about, let alone try to explain to a child. However, as an absolute part of *all* life on earth, explaining a pet's death is an extremely important lesson in life for a child to learn.

Stay within the child's level of understanding. A toddler, for example, should *not* be told that "Spot went to sleep and will never wake up again," or the odds are you'll have a toddler with screaming nightmares on your hands, or one that refuses to go to bed for fear of falling asleep and never waking up again.

It is okay to tell a very young child that "Spot died and went to heaven." Adding why Spot died, if that seems appropriate considering the cause of death and the age of the child. Regardless of your religious beliefs (or lack of them), the concept of a heavenly place with dogs and other pets is acceptable and satisfying to a youngster's peace of mind.

Avoid at all costs telling a savvy child an out-and-out lie. It does not help a child to cope with either the loss of a pet or with a healthy understanding of death if he or she is told "Spot has gone to live on a farm." Any bright child will immediately bounce back with, "Oh, good. When can we go and visit him?" Then you have to make up more lies. And in the long run, maybe years from now, a young adult will still harbor a grudge that he or she was not allowed to grieve over the death of a favorite dog. Young children are amazingly adept at coping with grief and with death when they are told the truth.

There are appropriate ways to explain the actual death. For instance, if the dog was getting on in years, a simple explanation to a young child might be, "Spot was very old and simply got to the end of his life. We were lucky to have had him with us for so long. And he was lucky that he had a happy life as your special friend."

Perhaps the dog was killed by a car, in which case you obviously don't want to dwell on the gory details, but you can certainly make a point about the danger of dogs running loose and of oncoming cars (and the up-side of leashes and holding hands, etc.).

Then there's the sick dog. This has to be treated carefully in the case of a very young child, because at some point the child will be sick and there's no reason to add fright to illness. Explain it with something like, "Spot was very sick with a disease that some dogs get. The doctors did everything they could, but Spot was so sick they couldn't save him."

An older child will probably want more details. A good way to handle it is to answer the questions without embroidering the facts. If you try to soften the blow, or explain more than was actually asked, you risk burdening the child with confusion.

WHAT NEXT?

No matter how the dog died, or what explanation you give, or how your child accepts it, the next step is crucial. Let your child (of any age) grieve for the dog. Even very young kids go through the same phases of grief that adults do on the death of a close family member. There is shock and initial sadness, followed by guilt (the "if I had done this or that" stage), and then anger ("Why me, why my dog?") and denial ("seeing" the dog, stepping over it, hearing a bark, etc.), and finally the acceptance of the separation and of death. Don't hide your own sorrow, and let the children know they can and should express their feelings openly.

This is no time for Daddy to say to a five-year-old, "Big boys don't cry." *They do, and they should.* If a child doesn't express any reaction at all, you might want to do a little probing to get him started. He may be stuck in guilt and hiding a vague notion that he was to blame for the pet's death. You want to dispel that idea as fast as you can. When an older child is undergoing treatment for a stress-related illness, parents are often surprised to learn of the profound effect a pet's death had on their child many years before. The parents either just never thought to ask the kids at the time how they felt, or didn't allow them to grieve openly.

Parental Explanations and Courses of Action

Bring up in general conversation your own sadness over Spot's death. You might bring up some funny little thing the dog used to do in order to show how much *you* already miss him, and then encourage the child to express his or her own feelings and memories.

There are two more things you can do to help your children manage the death of a pet, especially when this is the child's first encounter with the final phase of life. One is to organize a funeral with

A simple funeral for their pet lets the children say a final goodbye.

input from the kids. Not a giggly spoof, but a serious, dignified burial ceremony.

If it's possible to bury the pet or the ashes on your property, let the kids participate: digging the grave if they are capable of that, or decorating the grave if that's as much as they can do. Many a beloved pet has gone to its reward beneath a bunch of wilted, hand-picked dandelions. Maybe your kids aren't old enough to come up with a wordy eulogy, but encourage them to say goodbye even if it's a simple "Goodbye, Spot. You were a neat dog and we'll miss you." A funeral helps children to accept our normal custom following the death of a person or how we say a final goodbye. As parents, you will have set a good example in giving the life cycle a dignified ending.

I said there were two things to be done. First is the funeral and second is to *put off* getting another dog. Grieving is good; it is a natural healing process and you need to get it out of the house before inviting another dog in. Well-meaning friends often try to make up the loss to a child by promising (or worse, arriving at the door with) a new dog. No dog can be "replaced."

In our throwaway society, you can make a caring statement: We don't bury one dog and run out to buy another, the way we would replace a tube of toothpaste. A lot of thought must go into selecting a dog that will spend the next ten to fifteen years as a member of the family.

A new dog should come into your home with his/her own personality and idiosyncracies to occupy a very special place in your home and heart. It should not have to compete with the ghost of the previous resident. You may decide on a very different breed of dog, and your kids may now be old enough to have some ideas of their own.

Puppy Agility only takes reassurance in the beginning. It's a real confidence-builder.

11

What Dogs and Kids Can Do

FOR ALL YOU DISTRAUGHT parents—and bored kids—here are some answers to that dreaded wail, "There's nothing to do." Fortunately (for parents, kids and the dogs) there are so many different things to do with dogs that it's possible to go out on a limb and say, "Yes, indeed, there *is* something for everyone."

Start with Obedience, because you can't do *anything* with an unruly, untrained, unresponsive, distrusting, disrespectful dog! Obedience *competition* for most children is probably too highly competitive today beyond the first level for the Companion Dog title, and even that is really only for older unflappable kids. For the future, kids who have enjoyed training their own dogs might think about a career as an instructor or running an Obedience school.

AGILITY

Once the dog is trained, responds, trusts and so forth, the horizons really open up. At the top of the list, because it's the most fun, is Agility. This is a fairly new activity open to all breeds (pure and mixed) and is definitely the canine sport of the future. The idea was borrowed from the horse show jumping courses, with obstacles added that are unique to canine capabilities and that determine a dog's flexibility, fitness and ability to follow instructions. After the dog has learned how to overcome each type of obstacle, the owner/handler becomes a sort of cruise director on the course, and the dog does the work.

For both kids and dogs, Agility is sort of like being turned loose in a junkyard. There are hanging tires to jump through, numerous hurdles to jump over, sticks in the ground to slither in and out of, open-ended barrels to scrunch into and tunnel through, some with an added cloth tunnel (collapsed) to push and poke your way through, a plank to walk, an A-frame to climb up one side and down the other. Oh, it's obvious why this is Star's idea of heaven! Kids love it because there is so much action and because it *is* like a kids' playground.

This is not something to occupy dog and child for just a couple of days or weeks. It takes time to teach Star how to maneuver each obstacle before putting any two of them together, but for a somewhat older child who is able to operate as a team with the dog, this is a fun challenge. It is also something you can do at home.

There are two excellent books, *Agility Training—The Fun Sport for All Dogs,* by Jane Simmons-Moake and *Enjoying Dog Agility—From Backyard to Competition,* by Julie Daniels, that guide parents and kids step-by-step, with complete instructions for competitors of all ages and ability levels.

Agility is a "positive reinforcement" training exercise. There are no "No's" so that Star is assured of success. If she goofs up, the owner/trainer must assume he or she did not get the message across properly and they begin again. It's a method that is particularly good for children, for them to see that goof-ups do not eliminate self-esteem.

Needless to say, this is an exceptionally active sport and therefore requires an obedient dog and adult supervision at home, at least in the beginning. The number of Agility training groups is expanding rapidly nationwide, as are the competitions. This is a great spectator sport and one of the few where the spectators are encouraged to participate with shouts and applause. The dogs, like all good athletes, perform even better with an appreciative audience.

HURDLES, FLY-BALL, FRISBEE

Staying with an Obedience club can take you into fun activities, too. Hurdles are a favorite, and competitive hurdle races are often put on as demonstrations at dog shows. The fly-ball aspect can be added to the hurdles.

Fly-ball is a box with a pedal in front which the dog is taught to hit with a paw in order to release a spring that pops a tennis ball into the air for the dog to catch. Dogs have come up with many amusing variations on what they are supposed to do in this game!

National competition also takes place for the art (and it is an art!) of throwing a Frisbee in intricate tosses for a very clever and agile Star

Using a Floppy Disc is fun exercise for dogs and kids of any age.

to catch with equally intricate leaps. Again, at competition level, it is definitely for the teenagers, but for safety and just as much fun, there's a toy called the Soft Bite Floppy Disc, which is made of nylon with a soft, padded edge so neither the dog nor the child can be hurt. It is particularly good for dogs that are hesitant about taking hard sticks or wooden dumbbells in their mouths.

BREED-SPECIFIC FUN

Every breed of dog was genetically engineered to perform a specific job. I grant you, there's not much exciting activity if you're only training a lapdog to be a lapdog, but many of the Toy breeds do exceptionally well in Obedience and Agility.

Any dog can be taught to track, and there is no age barrier. Puppies learn to track and kids virtually go along for the ride, because once the course is laid out and instructions given, there isn't a whole lot to do but follow your dog. The exciting part is to see how accurate the dog is. For a child who becomes involved in **tracking**, it can lead to adult work with Search and Rescue (The American Rescue Dog Association). These are the people who are immediately on the scene of natural disasters (earthquakes, hurricanes, avalanches, etc.) and involved in locating lost hikers. The dogs and handlers able to do those dangerous and difficult jobs require very special training, but it all begins at this beginner level in a field with Rufus.

Herding breeds require a lot of training. In fact, the dogs that work for their living at what the rest of us consider sport are often trained by the shepherd and by older dogs. However, "part-time" workers may start out with ducks or sheep and have fun doing it, eventually going on to competition.

Hunting tests include a variety of hunting dogs and are definitely for older teenagers since this requires intensive training. However, there is also "Beagling," which can be exhausting because it is hunting on foot through fields, but it's fun and young pups learn with the pack.

Lure Coursing for sighthounds (Greyhounds, Afghans, Borzois, etc.) is very exciting and requires no particular training or skill on the part of the owner. At practice sessions, other breeds may be allowed to participate.

For all the small-to-medium-sized terriers, and for all Dachshunds (standard and mini, smooth, long or wirehaired), there are **Working Terrier Trials**. This is another of those "learn on the job" sports. No experience needed. The dogs are put on the ground sixteen feet from the opening of a ten-foot man-made tunnel in the earth at the end of which there is a small cage containing a rat. (The cage protects both dog and rat from each other.) When the dog reaches the rat it must behave like a terrier—bark, dig, scratch, etc. Each portion of the trial is timed, and a perfect score, as at the other trials mentioned, earns an award.

All these events are all-day outdoor activities. Some ask you to bring a picnic lunch, others have food available. Children of all ages are welcome but must be under the same control and supervision (of their parents) as the dogs. There would be mayhem if kids started playing active, noisy games distracting the dogs at work.

THE TEN THROUGH SEVENTEEN "JUNIORS"

Showing dogs in Junior Showmanship classes is for boys and girls, ages ten to seventeen. The procedure is as in breed conformation, not Obedience, but the juniors are judged only on how well they handle (or "show") the dog and how well they follow the instructions of the judge. No judgment is made of the dog.

The event sometimes suffers from stage mothers and fathers, but apart from that, the kids present a very nice picture of what parents want their kids to be: courteous, neatly dressed, clean and attractive, intent on the job at hand, following directions. (Whoa! Are these our kids we're talking about? Yes, indeed!)

Here again we can see the child/dog parallel. The child is treated with respect and learns to respect. The child is trusted and proves to be trustworthy. The child is taught what the job entails, learns from mistakes (and is not punished for them) and from the rewards of success, thus gaining self-confidence. Corrections are meted out calmly and politely, and praise is given lavishly and truthfully. The child learns to follow directions by listening carefully. This is a highly competitive activity (even without the parents' interference), but the child learns to handle triumph and defeat—we hope with equal moderation.

Junior Showmanship requires teamwork. Listening to the judge and looking just as nice as your dog.

In each of these instances you could substitute "dog" for "child." Perhaps that is why it works so well, because for the purposes of Junior Showmanship, the dog and handler need to become one entity, one picture, one team. The learning experience is the same for the dog and the child, right down to the winning and losing. Dogs aren't known to brag when they get a blue ribbon, nor do they carp when they lose. Maybe we can all learn humility from our dogs.

Junior Showmanship holds a future for the youngster who enjoys the sport and wants to work with and around dogs. Most begin by apprenticing to an established professional handler, and full-time jobs include kennel operation (show dog kennels, breeding or boarding kennels), breeding, grooming and training. Most of these can also be highly successful hobbies that start in the teens and can continue into retirement. "I've been in dogs all my life" is a proud statement often heard coming from a senior citizen.

Single-breed clubs may offer junior memberships. Their activities range from an awards dinner once a year to monthly newsletters,

A Junior is showing the judge she knows how to set her dog up on the table the way all small dogs are shown.

nationwide specialty shows, social get-togethers, and most exchange information with similar clubs in other countries around the world. The "world of dogs" can truly open up a whole lifetime of interests. Go anywhere in the world on vacation or business and you'll find dogs, breeders, handlers, dog shows, trials . . . well, you get the idea.

AKC "GOOD DOG" AWARD

The American Kennel Club now offers a certificate for dogs that pass the Canine Good Citizen test (which is given by many show-giving and Obedience clubs. It is for anyone, including older children, who can maintain good control of the dog under a variety of distractions using just basic Obedience training. This is not for a young child with a large, easily distracted dog, but the trainer will be able to say at what point both dog and partner are ready for such a test. It could be a very proud moment for a child.

PET SITTER

A first job involving dogs, and other pets perhaps, is that of pet sitting. Although this idea has been around for a long time with kids asking to walk or feed a neighbor's dog to earn a little pocket money, this is a new adult field of business. It is still something that responsible kids can do. Parents and the dog's owner are the best judges of how much responsibility any individual child can assume, but as a first business venture, it's a natural for many kids who have proven they can look after their own dog.

There are two good reasons why the services of pet sitters are needed. One is the fact that many dogs are left alone all day while their owners are at work. The second reason is that a number of dogs are, as we have discussed, "child substitutes." I know several in this last category who regularly hire a sitter to come into the home and actually sit with the dog if the owner goes to a movie or out for the evening! It is not unusual. To prove the point, there are several regional sitter businesses, and even a National Association of Pet Sitters.

Dog walking is another, separate occupation that can start in preteen years. This is a well-known profession in cities where dogs must be walked during the day for owners who work. It's quite a sight to see someone in New York City walking eight or ten dogs at once. A child, even a capable child, should not be asked to walk more than one at a time.

MISCELLANEOUS OCCUPATIONS AND ACTIVITIES

Future employment and college scholarships are available in diverse areas of the dog world. For example, all-breed dog clubs often donate a portion of their dog show gate for scholarships to universities offering degrees in veterinary medicine or research. Dog Writers Association of America offers scholarship awards to aspiring young journalists.

The hobby of being involved with dogs can lead to training dogs for the handicapped, which can range from raising a puppy that will become a guide dog for the blind, to training dogs for the deaf or those in wheelchairs, as well as for others with specific physical disabilities.

Going on Vacation
Don't know what to do with
The pet that needs...
T.L.C.?

Well you found it!
*Will take care of...

· dogs
· cats
· fish
· birds
· gerbil
· rabbits
· many more

*CAN provide references
Upon request

*For more information, ask
for Jennifer, at 226-8899.

My neighbor's first business flyer. She was so good at playing with puppies, she added it to her list.

Dogs as therapists. This young boy shares the pleasure of every youngster who takes their dog for a walk.

Or you can become part of a growing network of people who take their own trained (calm, well-mannered) therapy dogs to visit the sick, the elderly, the lonely. Therapy dogs perform the kind of small miracles you think are rare when you read about them, but are almost routine in hospices and nursing homes. A patient who hasn't spoken for months or years suddenly carries on a long conversation with a therapy dog; another who hasn't been able to use arms or hands "miraculously" holds and strokes a small canine visitor. It happens all the time. This is a job for the future, for a sensitive child to aspire to, because in reality each visit takes a great deal out of the dogs as well as their owners.

Accompanying Rufus to the vet's office might spark goals of becoming a veterinarian. There are almost as many branches of small and large animal medicine as there are for humans, including all the areas of research. Study of canine behavior is of interest to kids because it looks into all the possible answers to "why does Rufus do . . ." And if, when the time approaches, the years of study seem daunting,

Rollerblading is good exercise for athletes like this boy and his dog.

it's possible to become a certified technician and work with a veterinarian as a qualified assistant.

Town and municipal shelters as well as private ones always are in need of volunteer help and often take on trainees in the summer months.

A child who is adept at training Rufus beyond Obedience commands and is into tricks might be tempted to contemplate a career as an animal trainer for television or films.

Grooming is another profession open to young men and women. After attending grooming school, some go to work in kennels, some in established grooming shops, others start their own business. There is international competition for groomers, too.

Healthy dogs are good companions for roller blading (but keep your speed down to a comfortable level for the dog). Hiking is another recreation that's more fun with a dog along. Check your hiking area to be sure dogs are allowed; some are, some aren't and some only if kept on-leash. And take along water for Rufus.

Any kid who is into physical fitness can put Rufus through his exercises at the same time. How? Put Rufus on a Sit opposite you, then as you change from one routine to the next, tell Rufus ''Down,'' then ''Sit,'' then ''Down,'' ''Sit''—canine sit-ups!

12

Questions Kids Ask

 M AYBE I'm just a little prejudiced, but I think kids who like dogs are great letter writers! No long-winded explanations or excuses about a behavioral problem. They get right to the point. They are also good artists and many letters are embellished by pen-and-ink sketches of the dog in question.

Here's a sampling of kids' letters and my answers.

REGGIE

"I am a young dog owner (11). My dog Reggie ignores me. I feed him, take him outside to play and run, I give him baths, I groom him. All my Mom does is play with him sometimes. Reggie loves her. He lays next to her on the couch. How can I get Reggie to love me more?"

The dog likes each of you, but in different ways, for different reasons. He likes you for all the fun, active stuff you do together, and no doubt because you feed him. He recognizes your mother as the Number One person in your family and that is his way of showing her.

My dog Reggie
a miniature schnauzer

THE ENGLISH SETTLER AND CHUCKLES

"I am ten. My 1 dog is 4. He is part Chesapeak, part English Settler [*sic*]. He's as big as a colt. The other dog is 1 year and 6 days and I got Chuckles at 3 months. He runs around the house barking. He barked right into my friend's ear—loud. He chews up all my socks, and Kleenex. Two more things. He does not lift his leg, and he does not climb stairs. Is that normal? He is a lot of fun and we love him."

Males begin to lift a leg anywhere from eight weeks to two years. Your puppy knows stairs are dangerous (scary, too) so he's being cautious. Give him time and if he doesn't catch on, teach him very slowly with lots of treats, using your body (sitting on each step) to give him confidence.

As for chewing up socks and tissues, the pup can only chew them if he can get ahold of them. Keep tissues out of his reach (used ones should be thrown away) and keep your clean socks in your drawer and dirty ones in the laundry hamper. (Now I'm beginning to sound like your mother, aren't I?)

Plan to take Chuckles to Obedience classes soon. Active dogs, with active minds, enjoy learning to do things that please you. You'll have fun, too.

196

CAMPUS ORATOR

"I live on the school campus where my Dad works and I own an exceptionally calm English Spring Spanial [*sic*] two years old. She has just started barking at students going by in the morning when I let her out. Hats bother her, too. She even barked at my Dad when he wore one.

"Dad yells at the dog when she barks, and so does my Mom. I don't think that's the right thing to do. Can you help in this prediciment? [*sic*]"

The dog has to be *taught* not to bark. Yelling makes some dogs bark more because they think the person is "barking," too. Take her out on a loose leash in the morning and just follow her around. Praise her *as* she relieves herself.

If she barks, say immediately, "No bark," and call her to you, or toss her a toy, or run in another direction to distract her. Tell her "Good girl" as she stops barking and comes to you. The other thing to do is to get the dog out (on-leash, of course) among other people, bicycles, dogs, men in hats and so forth. How about Obedience classes?

MISGUIDED COMFORT

"My mother said to write you about my dog. He liked everyone until he was about one year old. Then he decided he didn't like kids anymore, at least none of my friends. My parents hold him and comfort him when kids come over, but he still snaps at them. So now we have to keep him in one room or my mother holds him on her lap. What can we do? (He was neutered.)"

Holding and comforting tells the dog that you approve of whatever is being done at the time. So, without meaning to, your parents have encouraged the dog's dislike of children. At about one year, lots of dogs turn into teenagers and need a firm hand. It's not too late. Get him into an Obedience class with a firm, but friendly, instructor and explain the problem. Only when the instructor says the dog is ready should you begin to reintroduce the dog to kids with the dog on a Sit-Stay.

A THANK-YOU NOTE

This one came from a ten-year-old girl whose dog was greatly overweight because of the two most common causes: She was overfed and underexercised.

"Nicca and I would like to thank you for sending us the diet. We didn't know how to make her lose weight. Your way really works and Nicca has already lost six pounds. She looks a lot better and is happier. We will let you know how she does."

Thank-you notes are nice.

4-H OBEDIENCE

"I take my year-old Maltese to 4-H Obedience class, but my dog can't catch up with me when we go in circles. My leader says to keep practicing. What can I do?

"Also, tell other kids about 4-H because the Obedience is free and they have shows, too. You can even have a mixed breed!"

If you are in a class with bigger dogs, stay at the end of the line and go at your dog's own speed. A Maltese can move really fast for a small dog, but it's not a race. You need to set *your* pace so that your dog is able to keep up with you comfortably whether you're walking down the street or in the class.

Thank you for the information on the 4-H Extension Service. Some do charge a small fee, especially if they hand out booklets or other materials.

THE ROUNDBUNKISH PUP

Some are better spellers than others! (But at least this little girl tried.)

"Hi! My dog has been a roundbunkish dog since he was a pup. We used to play ruff [*sic*] with him. He's been biting people. If we doan't [*sic*] stop it, he'll be put to sleep. How can I get him to stop bitting [*sic*]."

198

Billy is learning a lot about taking reponsibility for all his animals as well as learning about dog Obedience.

Rambunctious dogs are hard to train, but if the dog has already bitten more than once, you should not handle the problem yourself. Seek professional help, but it's still possible the dog will have to be put to sleep.

PLEASE, MAY I HAVE A DOG?

This one got my attention.

"I do not have a pet, but I am trying to change that. I have been begging my parents for a dog ever since I was 4 and now I am 10. I've tried every possible way to convince my parents that we need a dog. Once I came so, so close, but when we went to get the dog, it was gone. I don't know what happened, but now my parents won't allow me to have a dog. Please help me convince them we need one?"

She's at the right age, has wanted a dog for a long time, doesn't mention siblings so may be an only child. At the time, I suggested she find the real reason her parents said no. If money was a problem, adopting a dog from a shelter or rescue service might help. If it was training, she should look into 4-H or other classes. That was then. Of course *now* I would tell her to give her parents a copy of this book!

SCARED, LONELY PUP

Another parental problem.

"I have a black Lab puppy whose name is Zoe. I mostly take care of her. I am 10. She barks at night and keeps us up. My Dad has to get up at 3 in the morning to go to work and needs his sleep. I bring Zoe into my room at night so he can sleep. How can we stop her from barking all night outside?"

The puppy is lonely and frightened to be left outside all night. Besides, she'd rather be with you, and if you let her in sometimes when she barks, she'll keep on barking. Dogs are *companion* animals and puppies especially are upset when left alone outdoors at night.

Why not let her sleep in your room until she's fully grown (about two years)? Labradors make very good students, so take Zoe to Obedience classes as soon as you can.

A WIRED TERRIER!

This dog should have been named for a hurricane!

"I have a cute little wired terrier named Bumper, 4 months old. We've been training her for two months. Every time we tell her to do something, she ignores us. She breaks glasses, knocks over tables and chairs. If she wants to go outside, she'll go, but if she doesn't, she won't. Will she be like this all her life?"

To answer the last question first, yes, if you let her. She certainly is "wired"! Four months is very young, but not too young to learn. She's not ignoring you; she just hasn't yet learned what it is you want her to do. Get into Kindergarten Puppy Training—fast.

Index

202